Russian Dwarf Ha

Russian Dwarf Hamsters as pets.

Russian Dwarf Hamster book including care, pros and cons, housing, cost, diet and health.

By

Macy Peterson

Table of Contents

Introduction

I want to thank you and congratulate you for buying the book 'Dwarf hamster as a pet'. This book will help you to understand everything you need to know about domesticating a dwarf hamster. You will learn all the aspects related to raising the animal successfully at home. You will be able to understand the pros and cons, behaviour, basic care, breeding, keeping, housing, diet and health issues related to the animal.

If you wish to own a dwarf hamster or even if you already own one, it is important to understand the basic characteristics of the animal. You should know what you can expect from the animal and what you can't. This will help you to tweak the way you behave with the dwarf hamster in the household, which in turn will help to build a strong bond between the pet and you.

Domestication of an animal has its unique challenges and issues. If you are not ready for these challenges, then you are not ready to domesticate the animal. It is important that you understand that owning any pet will have its advantages and disadvantages.

A pet is like a family member. You will be more like a parent than like a master to the pet. You will be amazed to see how much love and affection your dwarf hamster will give through his ways and actions. But, for that to happen you have to make sure that the animal is taken care of. The animal should be loved in your household. If your family is not welcoming enough for the pet, the animal will lose its sense of being very quickly.

The diet of the dwarf hamster will have a direct effect on the way he feels and functions. As the owner of the pet, it will be your responsibility that the pet is fed the right food in the right amounts and at the right times. You will also have to make sure that the pet is safe and secure at all times. It is important that you learn about the common health issues that a dwarf hamster is likely to suffer from. This will help you to avoid these health conditions and keep the dwarf hamster safe.

If the dwarf hamster does not feel wanted and loved in your home, you will see a decline not just in its behaviour but also its health. This is the last thing that you should do to an animal. An animal deserves as much love and protection as a human being. You should be able to provide the pet a safe and sound home. Your family should be caring towards the pet. You have to be like a parent to the dwarf hamster. This is the basic requirement when planning to bring an animal home.

If you have already bought or adopted a dwarf hamster, even then you need to understand your pet so that you take care of him in a better way. You should see whether with all its pros and cons, the animal fits well into your household. Domesticating and taming a pet is not only fun. There is a lot of hard work that goes into it.

Once you form a relationship with the dwarf hamster, it gets better and easier for you as the owner. The pet will grow up to be friendly and adorable. He will also value the bond as much as you do. This will be good for the pet and also for you as the pet owner in the long run. It is important that you are ready to commit before you decide to domesticate the animal. If you are a prospective buyer, then understanding of these points will help you to make a wise decision.

When you bring a pet home, it becomes your responsibility to raise the pet in the best way possible. You have to provide physically, mentally, emotionally and financially for the pet. All these points are not being discussed to frighten or scare you. In fact, these points are being discussed to make you understand that you have to know the right ways to domesticate a dwarf hamster. If the animal establishes a trust factor with you, he will always remain loyal to you. This is a great quality to have in a domesticated animal.

The pet will actually surprise you with their intelligence and smartness. This makes the pet all the more endearing. His unique ways and antics will leave you and the entire family in splits. If you have had a bad day, your pet will surely help you to release all the tension and enjoy life. If you are looking for a pet that is affectionate, lovable and fun, then the dwarf hamster is the ideal choice for you as they won't disappoint you.

If you are looking forward to raising a dwarf hamster as a pet, there are many things that you need to understand before you can domesticate the animal. You need to make sure that you are ready in terms of the right preparation. There are certain unique characteristics of the animal that make him adorable, but these traits can also be very confusing for many people. You can't domesticate the animal with all the confusions in your head.

There are still many doubts regarding their domestication methods and techniques. There are many things that the prospective owners don't understand about the animal. They find themselves getting confused as to what should be done and what should be avoided. If you are still contemplating whether you wish to buy a dwarf hamster or not, then it is important that you understand all about the maintenance of the pet, so that you can make the right choice for yourself. This book will help you make that decision.

This book is meant to equip you with all the knowledge that you need to have before buying the dwarf hamster and bringing it home. This book will help you understand the basic behaviour and antics of the animal. You will also learn various tricks and tips. These tips and tricks will be a quick guide when you are looking for different ways to have fun with your pet.

It is important that a prospective buyer has all the important information regarding a dwarf hamster. You need to make sure that you are ready in terms of the right preparation. This book will help you in this preparation and be a better owner for your pet.

You will learn many ways to take care of your dwarf hamster. This book will try to address every question that you might have when looking at raising the animal. You will be able to understand the pet and give it the care that it requires.

You can expect to learn the pet's basic behaviour, eating habits, shelter requirements, breeding, grooming and training techniques among other important things. In short, the book will help you to be a better owner by learning everything about the animal. This will help you form an everlasting bond with the pet.

Chapter 1: What are Russian Dwarf hamsters?

In the 1970s, the dwarf hamster was introduced in many parts of Europe. The have gained a lot of popularity amongst pet lovers across the world since the time of their introduction.

It is known that the dwarf hamster is a wonderful pet, especially for adults and older children. This hamster will prove to be a great companion if you are looking for one.

But, the animal, like most other animals will require you to understand this unique temperament. This will help you to take care of the pet well in all conditions.

Syrian hamsters are very popular across the world. The dwarf hamster is said to be about half the size of Syrian one. These dwarf animals look very cute and adorable to one and all.

The Syrian hamsters are known to hibernate. But, as the parent of the dwarf hamster you don't have to worry about this. The dwarf hamsters are accustomed to cold weather. They are not known to hibernate in the wild or even in captivity.

One physical feature that is quite glaring in the dwarf hamsters is the stuffed cheeks. The head of the dwarf hamster looks quite large in comparison to tits body.

The truth is that the dwarf hamster has cheek pouches. These pouches allow the hamster to save food in them. The hamster will mostly have its cheeks full.

1. Types of dwarf hamsters

If you are looking to hand raise a dwarf hamster, then it is important that you know that there are basically three kinds of dwarf hamsters.

- Roborovski dwarf hamsters

- Winter white dwarf hamster

- Campbell's dwarf hamster

The last two categories, the Winter white dwarf hamster and the Campbell's dwarf hamster are together known as Russian dwarf hamsters.

It is also quite interesting that there are many hybrid varieties of the dwarf hamsters available. The hybrids are mostly produced by the last two categories of the dwarf hamster.

There is another species that is more of a rat and less of a hamster and is called the Chinese dwarf hamster. It should be mentioned here that this species is not related to the three kinds of dwarf hamsters.

This section will help you to understand the three types of dwarf hamsters well.

Roborovski dwarf hamsters

Roborovski dwarf hamsters are quite popular as pets. They are also called Robo dwarf hamsters. These animals are found in various areas, such as Northern China, Kazakhstan and Russia.

This species of hamster is the smallest in size. A fully grown adult will be less than three inches.

If you are worried about the diet of these animals, then there is nothing to worry about. They can eat vegetables, fruits, grains, meat and insects.

These animals are very fast and energetic. The nocturnal animal runs on an average of 100 miles per night. This is the amount of energy that they have.

This species of hamster has a whitish underbelly. The animal is grey brown in colour. There are a few hamsters that have a white face. These hamsters are called White face robo dwarf hamsters or Husky robo dwarf hamsters.

Most dwarf hamsters have dorsal stripes. But, this particular species does not have these stripes.

These dwarf hamsters are ready for breeding in the first three to four months. A female is typically ready by the fourth month and the male dwarf hamster is ready by the third month.

The female is capable of producing five to six pups after a gestation period of about twenty two to thirty days.

The average life span of the animal is known to be three years. But, if you take good care of the dwarf hamster, it can live up to four years.

Russian dwarf hamsters

The last two categories, the Winter white dwarf hamster and the Campbell's dwarf hamster are together known as Russian dwarf hamsters. They are also called fancy Russian dwarf hamsters.

The Winter white dwarf hamster and the Campbell's dwarf hamster are known to have many similarities. There are many people that confuse these two species. It is important to study them well so that you understand how they differ from one another.

Winter white dwarf hamsters

Winter white dwarf hamsters are also quite popular as pets. These animals are found in various areas, such as Central Asia, Siberia and Russia.

The average life span of the animal in the wild is known to be one year. But, if you take good care of the dwarf hamster, it can live up to three years.

This species is referred to by various names, such as Djungarian hamster, White winter hamster and Siberian hamster. A fully grown adult of this species will be three to four inches in length.

The Winter white dwarf hamster is called so because the dwarf hamster has the unique quality to change its body colour of grey to white during severe winter. It should be noted that your pet hamster might not be able to change its colour because of artificial heat and light systems in the house.

These dwarf hamsters have dorsal stripes on their bodies. These animals come in many colours such as dark grey, sapphire pearl, pearl and marble. The belly of the hamster is white in colour.

These dwarf hamsters are ready for breeding when they are four to six months of age. The female is capable of producing four to eight pups after a gestation period of about eighteen to twenty five days. The female can also give birth to fourteen pups in the litter.

Campbell's dwarf hamsters

In appearance, the Campbell's dwarf hamster resembles the winter white dwarf hamster. This species is the most common of dwarf hamsters.

If you visit a pet store, you are likely to find this species in abundance. These animals are found in various areas, such as Central Asia, China and Russia.

The average life span of the animal is known to be one and a half years. But, if you take good care of the dwarf hamster, it can live up to two and a half years.

These dwarf hamsters have dorsal stripes on their bodies. These animals come in many colours such as dark grey, sapphire pearl, pearl and marble. The belly of the hamster is white in colour.

These dwarf hamsters are ready for breeding when they are three to four months of age. The female is capable of producing up to ten pups after a gestation period of about eighteen to twenty days.

2. Life span

The lifespan of a dwarf hamster is from one to four years. The three different species of pet dwarf hamsters differ in this regard. It is also known that most dwarf hamsters will only live till the age of three years.

As the owner, you should know this that your care will go a long way helping the dwarf hamster to live longer. Most of the dwarf hamsters rarely reach four years of age because they do not proper care.

The animal needs veterinarian care and medical attention if you expect him to live a healthy and long life. It is known that a dwarf hamster in the wild has a shorter life span as compared to the pet ones.

3. Where can you get a Russian dwarf hamster?

If you are planning to buy a dwarf hamster then you can do so from either a pet store or from a breeder. If a previous owner is giving up his dwarf hamster, then you can also take it from him.

Previously, it was mandatory for breeders to be registered with the International Hamster Registry, but it is not compulsory now. The owner himself can register if he wishes to.

But, a good breeder will always keep the healt and pedigree records of the pet up to date. A good breeder will also discourage the breeding of dwarf hamsters that have genetic problems.

You can also adopt the animal from a welfare home or from someone who is giving away the pet. This is a simple way to give an animal a new and caring home.

4. A male dwarf hamster or a female dwarf hamster?

If this question is bothering you, then you should know that it does not matter whether you buy a male dwarf hamster or a female.

The personality of your pet dwarf hamster will not depend on whether it is male or female. The difference is more to do with anatomy than behaviour.

In some smaller pets, the male members have a very peculiar smell which is stronger than the female members. But, this is not the case with the dwarf hamsters.

A female dwarf hamster will not have her period if that is one of your concerns because the female is an induced ovulator. It does not go into a period of heat.

The male will not have prominent testicles like many other male animals. Some males would masturbate quite often. This can be embarrassing for some owners.

It is believed that females are more prone to various reproductive diseases. But there are no real facts that can prove this. It is only based on the number of cases that get reported each year.

5. Advantages and disadvantages of domesticating a Russian dwarf hamster

It is important that you understand the challenges that come with domestication of animals such as the dwarf hamster.

Whenever you decide to domesticate an animal, there are always some advantages and disadvantages related to the keeping of the animal at home.

There could be many other important points and issues that should be discussed before making the final decision of the animal.

A few advantages and disadvantages of domestication of dwarf hamsters have been discussed in this section. If you are a prospective buyer, then this section will help you to make a wise decision.

If you have already bought a dwarf hamster, then this list of advantages and disadvantages will help you to prepare yourself for the challenges ahead.

Once you understand the areas that would require extra work from your side, you will automatically give your very best in those areas.

Advantages of domesticating a dwarf hamster:

There are many pros of domesticating a dwarf hamster. This animal can prove to be a great pet for your household if you raise him the right way. The various advantages of domesticating a dwarf hamster are as follows:

- Dwarf hamsters are very small in size. This makes them easy to handle. You don't have to worry about handling a huge and bulky pet.

- The dwarf hamster looks very different. They are popular for their exotic looks. The pet at your house will be the talking point of each and every visitor of the house.

- These animals are exotic and desired, and human beings are naturally attracted towards such animals.

- Pet dwarf hamsters have the habit of licking and cleaning themselves. This habit of the animal makes him similar to pets such as cats, which also lick and clean themselves.

- A dwarf hamster is a very sharp animal. It is always good to have a pet that is intelligent and sharp.

- You will not have to worry too much about the hygiene of the pet unlike many pets that require constant cleaning and grooming. This pet will not demand too much of your time in grooming it.

- If domesticated in the right way, they can grow to be entertaining and lovable animals. You will be delighted to see how much your pet will adore you with the passage of time.

- They are capable of forming great emotional bonds with their masters. This may require a great deal of effort and also time from your side.

- Though the dwarf hamster might take some time to interact well with the humans, they can be social and friendly in their demeanour. They will start recognising people from their scents.

- In case you domesticate a dwarf hamster, then you will not have to worry too much about the diet. The diet of the pet is similar to a pet dog or cat's diet. Also, there are many diet mixtures and pellets available commercially. These easily available food items ensure that the right nutrition is given to your pet.

- He will slowly get used to your scent and will associate it with security. This will help the two of you to bond well.

- The pet belongs to a class that does not require too much grooming. You don't have to give the dwarf hamster frequent baths. A healthy dwarf hamster will only need it few times a year. This is great news for owners who fear giving baths to pet animals.

- Many people believe that since these animals belong to the wild, they would be very difficult in their nature and it would be impossible to train them. But, this is not true. If you provide good training to your dwarf hamster, you will notice that he responds well.

- The dwarf hamsters are very soft and gentle in their nature. If the dwarf hamster is supervised, he will always have fun in certain limits. You will also get to see the calm, composed and gentle side of the animal.

- Many a times, when a young animal is rescued, it fails to survive. If you happen to rescue a young dwarf hamster, then the good news is that they can be hand raised.

- You would have to be extra careful and cautious while taking care of the young one, but when all the precautions are taken, it is a very much possible task to hand raise a rescued dwarf hamster.

- A dwarf hamster is a solitary animal. You don't have to worry about giving him company all the time. The animal will be very happy when he is left all alone to enjoy his own company.

- The animal does not need vaccinations like most other animals. This can be a great relief for you.

Disadvantages of domesticating a dwarf hamster:

While you have studied the advantages of domesticating a dwarf hamster, it is also important to learn about the various disadvantages that come along. Everything that has merits will also have some demerits, and you should be prepared for this.

The adorable animal has his own set of challenges when it comes to domesticating him. It is important to understand these disadvantages so that you can be better prepared for them.

Following are the disadvantages of raising a dwarf hamster:

- These animals have a very unique temperament, and it would require patience from your side to understand this kind of temperament. You will have to make an effort to understand why they behave the way they behave.

- The pet has a lifespan of 3-5 years. This can be a big disadvantage for many people. While you invest a lot of money and emotions on the pet, you will not be able to enjoy the emotional bond for a very long time.

- These animals sleep a lot. Though this can be an advantage for you, if you want a pet that will play with you all day, then you are in for a loss. The dwarf hamster will play with you when it wants to.

- The animal can gain weight very easily. Many dwarf hamsters are known to be suffering from obesity, which is not good for them.

- A lot of care has to be taken to ensure that they maintain good health. They catch disease causing bacteria and viruses very easily. Once infected, it is difficult to treat them.

- The dwarf hamster has a habit to bite. This is a habit that helps them to express what they are going through. Biting can hurt you, and the pet can deficate on you or your clothes. But you can train the dwarf hamster against such behaviour.

- The food that you serve them might be easily available, but the right brands might not be too cheap.

- Because of his energy levels, the dwarf hamster can run into things and can get hurt very easily.

- They are so small that you can lose them if you don't keep track of what they are doing. This is very important.

- The pet has a tendency to run into danger every now and then. You have to be very serious about proofing the house, else you will lose him.

- If the dwarf hamster is lost, it is very difficult to find him. He will not be able to find his way back to the house. And, the dwarf hamster is so small that anything can happen to him when he is lost.

- The animal can seek a lot of attention. Though the pet is solitary in its nature, there can be phases when he will require you to pamper him a lot.

- The pet can get stressed and depressed very easily. The pet is a defensive pet. He will get scared and stressed, but will not attack. This can affect him a lot.

- These animals love playing and running around. These pets are fond of exploring things. They can create a mess if not monitored.

- The dwarf hamsters are very noisy. These animals use different kinds of noises to communicate what they are feeling. This can get very difficult for the members of the family. They are definitely not suitable for someone who is looking for a quiet and calm pet.

- If spending too much money is an issue with you, then you will have to think twice before purchasing the animal.

- You should also understand the various other costs that you will encounter while raising your pet. You might have to spend a lot of money on their health.

- The dwarf hamster is very good in hiding sickness and illnesses. If you are not careful, you will miss the symptoms which can worsen the condition of a sick pet.

- It is known that the male dwarf hamster masturbates. This can be very embarrassing for a pet owner because the male will do it anywhere and anytime.

- Your pet dwarf hamster will not adapt too well to changing surroundings. You will have to make sure that you provide the animal with everything that he needs to live a good life.

- A dwarf hamster will also make a lot of noises. A dwarf hamster makes noises even when he is sleeping. This can be very worrisome for people who are not used to these pets and also for their family.

- Dwarf hamsters are very sensitive to various kinds of noises. You can't play loud music around them. It is even advised that you don't speak too loudly when they are around. Loud sounds can irritate them.

Chapter 2: Bringing the dwarf hamster home

A very big mistake that many new owners commit is that they buy a pet out of an impulse decision. They don't look into the pros and cons of domesticating the animal.

Just because one of your friends has a dwarf hamster does not mean that even you should have one. Just because your kids find the animal cute does not mean that you should have one.

Important decisions like domestication of an animal have to be based on proper understanding and research. You should be sure that you understand the requirements of the animal.

Domestication of an animal is a commitment that you should be able to fulfil at all times. You can't run away from it when you want. You need to be sure that you are ready.

You should also be sure that you understand your lifestyle in connection with the animal. Your lifestyle should support the animal and not disrupt his natural way of being.

When you are planning to domesticate the dwarf hamster, you should be sure that you are well prepared. There are some crucial points that you need to consider when planning to bring the dwarf hamster home.

1. Nocturnal animal

A dwarf hamster is a nocturnal animal. He will be awake during the most part of the night. Some owners try to change the pattern of the animal by trying to keep him awake during day time.

These owners miserably fail because it is almost impossible to change the nocturnal habits of the dwarf hamster. You will have to adjust and find a way around this habit.

If you are looking for an animal that would be the lifeline of the house during day time, then you are in for a disappointment.

If you are looking for an animal that will play around with the kids during their playtime, then the dwarf hamster is definitely not for you.

The pet will get irritated and grumpy if he is forced to get up during the times when he prefers to sleep. Every new owner should keep this in mind before going out to buy the animal.

It should be noted that if you forcefully try to alter the natural mechanism of the animal, you will put him in extreme danger.

Dwarf hamsters that are forced to eat at certain times and are forced to be awake during the daytime so that they sleep in the night have a high chance of acquiring various diseases.

Such dwarf hamsters will be battling stress and will fall sick frequently. The immune system of the animal will be low, thus making things worse.

Attempting to change the animal's natural cycle just for your convenience is the worst thing anyone can do. It is very cruel, and you should never do this to your pet.

It is better to avoid domesticating such an animal than to spoil his life and leave him stranded.

2. Introducing the dwarf hamster to a new dwarf hamster

If you have plans to buy more than one dwarf hamster, then you need to understand the best combinations for you. A dwarf hamster is an animal that does not look for company. He is happy being alone.

You should not assume that you can keep two dwarf hamsters in the same cage. There is a chance that the dwarf hamsters will not get along.

It is believed that a female dwarf hamster has a higher chance of getting along with another female. A male will not accept another male because of dominance issues.

You can also try the combination of a young dwarf hamster and an old dwarf hamster. Keeping the male dwarf hamster and the female dwarf hamster is ideal for serious breeders.

You have to be careful while introducing the dwarf hamsters to each other. The process has to be gradual and slow. Don't force them to stay with each other in the same cage.

You will have to take certain precautions. If you give some time to the pets, they might get along with the passage of time. And, this will also give you some time to understand how the dwarf hamsters are adjusting to each other.

There are a basic set of steps to make it easier for the pets. Dwarf hamsters could have territorial issues that you will have to address. Also, the new pet could carry some disease causing bacteria and viruses. You will have to make sure that the new dwarf hamster does not pass on these to the older one.

The first thing that you need to do when you are planning to bring a new dwarf hamster home is to get another cage for the dwarf hamster. You can get a simple cage for him because this will only be his temporary home. You should keep the new animal in this cage for a few weeks.

The new dwarf hamster will take some time to get adjusted to the new environment around him. The older dwarf hamster will be protected from any disease that the new dwarf hamster might be carrying.

It is important that you keep the cage of the new pet away from the older one. They should ideally be in separate rooms. It is critical that you observe a quarantine period of at least two weeks. These two weeks will help you to establish whether your new pet animal is healthy or not.

With the passage of time, if you witness your new pet to be unwell, you should take him to the vet. After the passage of the first few weeks, you can be sure that the new pet is not carrying any disease.

Now, it is time to slowly introduce the pets to each other. But, this has to be done in stages. You should understand that the older dwarf hamster is already used to a certain life style. He is used to a way of living and also to the people and pets around him.

He will try to fight it out with the new dwarf hamster to establish his supremacy. This fight for survival and supremacy will not only strain the relationship of the pets, but will also lead to a lot of stress in their individual lives.

To make the transition easier for both the dwarf hamsters, you should begin by introducing them to each other's smell. After the first few weeks of isolating them, bring their cages closer.

You can place the cage of the new dwarf hamster next to the cage of the older one in way that they can see each other and smell each other.

Another trick that you apply is that you can exchange the bedding of the two dwarf hamsters after a few days. This is a technique that will help them to identify each other's smell.

Once you see them acknowledging each other, you know it is time to introduce them in a more intimate way. You can now bring them together in an open space.

You will find them smelling and sniffing one another. This is the pets' way of introducing themselves. You need to supervise such meetings.

The introduction period could extend up to many days and weeks. You might also find your animals wrestling with each other. This would be accompanied by hissing sounds.

If you see a dwarf hamster bleeding or being too stressed and scared, then you know that it is time to intervene. You should also know that the age of the pets will also determine as to how well they get along.

If the pets seem to enjoy playing together, they will slowly start getting along. A strong indication that the pets are comfortable with each other is when they are curling up together.

But, if your animals are brutal towards each other and refuse to get along even after multiple trials, then you know that they need to be away from each other.

You will have to step in such extreme cases. In such a case you are advised to have two separate cages.

3. Precautions to be taken

You should understand that there are certain precautions that each owner should follow when domesticating a dwarf hamster. It is very important that you get acquainted with the dos and don'ts of keeping the animal.

You have to allow yourself the time to understand the behaviour, mannerisms, habits and moods of the pet. This will allow you avoid unpleasant incidents for your pet dwarf hamster.

This will help you and your family to be safe. And, this will also allow the pet dwarf hamster to be secure at all times.

Spotting a frightened and scared dwarf hamster

Your pet might get overwhelmed or scared by things around him. It is important to spot a scared pet if you wish to help him. The pet can easily get scared and go into depression.

It is easy to spot a scared dwarf hamster. If you see your dwarf hamster being pushed up in a corner, you should know that something is not right. If he is making noises similar to a hiss then you should know that he is definitely scared.

The fur or hair of the pet stands up as an act of self-defence. The pet will show less movement from his side.

It is important to know when your pet is scared so that you can comfort him and make him feel better. There are different ways to comfort different kinds of animals. For your dwarf hamster, you just need to reassure him.

Leave the pet alone for some time, but be in the vicinity so that you can keep a check on him. The pet should not get too stressed or scared. This is not good for his health.

The dwarf hamster is known to recover when you give him some care and warmth. He will know when the danger that frightened him is no longer there, and this will help him to go back to normal. If you really wish to help then speak a few kind words to your pet.

Take him in your arms and comfort him. Put him on your lap and pet him. Just speak a few kind words to reinforce the fact that everything is fine and then just leave the dwarf hamster for some time. This works for a scared dwarf hamster.

Precautions at home

As the owner of the dwarf hamster, you have to make sure that you take all the necessary precautions to keep everything under control. There are many obvious and necessary precautionary steps that you would need to exercise.

The enclosure should be built keeping in mind all the necessary safety measures. Apart from these measures, you would also have to take certain precautions as the owner of the dwarf hamster.

As the owner, it is important that you are aware of your pet's whereabouts at all times. This will allow you to know if the pet is up to some mischief or not.

As the owner of the dwarf hamster, you have to be well prepared. Not all animals are the same, so this makes your task more challenging. When you bring your pet home, start out very slowly with him. Look for his reactions for everything that you do. This will help you to understand what your pet enjoys and what he does not enjoy.

An important point that you should note is that you should never force your pet to do anything. If he does not enjoy a belly rub, there should be no reason for you to force the rubs on him. Allow him to enjoy what he genuinely enjoys.

When your pet is very young, start out with rubbing around his ears. Make sure that you are as gentle as possible. You shouldn't hurt the pet in any way. Slowly rub other parts of his body.

But, each time you try something new, look for the pet's reactions. If you think that he is not enjoying himself then avoiding petting those particular areas.

Precautions with children

If you have children at home, then you need to train your children along with training the animal. The children need to be taught about the nature of the pet.

Firstly, you need to teach the children to allow the pet to be the way he wants to be. The kid might want to play with the dwarf hamster, but the dwarf hamster could be sleeping. The children need to be taught not to disturb the pet.

Kids can sometimes pull or push the pet around. The child might just be trying to be a little friendly or naughty, but the dwarf hamster can get irritated. The pet might get severely stressed and might withdraw from everything.

You should keep children below the age of five away from the pet. The simple reason for this is that smaller kids will not understand how to behave with the pet.

The kids of this age will not know the limits that they shouldn't cross with the dwarf hamster. Even if they are under adult supervision, there are high chances of a mishap. This will mean that both the kids and pet dwarf hamster will become a danger for each other.

You should make sure that the older children play with the pet only under your supervision or some adult supervision. You should have a discussion with the kid as to how the dwarf hamster is different from the rest of the pets.

You should also make sure that you don't scare your child away. You need to inform him for his own safety.

4. Russian Dwarf hamster with other animals

A dwarf hamster is a defensive animal. He will not attack even when he is being attacked. If you have bigger animals at home, there is a chance that the dwarf hamster might get hurt.

Your dwarf hamster is solitary in nature. He does not need company. There is no need to force your pet to get along with other pet animals.

But, if you already have other pets and you want them to at least try to get along then you will have to take certain precautions. You should remember that you can't force anything. You also need a lot of patience.

When you first introduce your pets to each other, you need to be extra cautious. In the beginning, keep the pets away from each other, but in the same vicinity so that they can identify with each other's smell.

It is important to note that even if the pets in the household seem friendly and cordial to each other, you should make sure that there is some supervision when they are together.

You never know when they get hostile towards each other. You should never leave your dwarf hamster alone with any other animal. This can be very dangerous.

Other pets in the home

If you have other pets in your home, then that will be an important point of consideration while you are planning for your new dwarf hamster.

Firstly, you should consider the space that you are left with. After your other pets take up their space, are you left with additional space for the dwarf hamster?

Secondly, do you have the energy to look after another pet? You should make an attempt to understand your routine better. Do you find yourself pressed for time?

Do you struggle to take care of the pets that you currently have? Do you sometimes wish that you could get rid of the pets? These questions will help you to decide whether you have the energy for another pet or not.

If you are sure that you have the space and the energy to keep another pet, then the next point that needs your attention is the number and the type of pets that you already have.

It is known that if ferrets and dogs are in the vicinity of a dwarf hamster, the dwarf hamster can have a really difficult time. The smell of these animals can be unbearable for a dwarf hamster.

It is also known that bigger animals, such as cats, have a tendency to terrorize an animal such as dwarf hamsters. The cat might just be curious, but that can scare your pet dwarf hamster.

5. Proofing the home

A dwarf hamster can be a very curious pet. You might be busy with some work, and before you know your pet might be walking into some real danger.

The dwarf hamster is so small that you might not know where he is most of the time. This makes it very important that you understand the behaviour of your pet very well.

The pet can accidentally injure himself. The damage could be serious and irrevocable. He can also cause damage to the property of the house. You can't change the personality of an animal, but there are other things you can do.

A simple solution to keep your pet safe and the house safe is to pet proof your home. This section will discuss the potential dangers to the dwarf hamsters and also some simple ways to proof your house.

There is no use crying after the damage has been done. It is always better to take the necessary precautions in the very beginning. This section will help you to understand the various ways to proof your home.

You should make sure that all liquid chemicals are far away from the pet animal. If a chemical is in reach of the pet, he might accidently spill it all over him. You should make sure that all such supplies are kept in top cabinets where the pet can't reach.

If a dwarf hamster climbs into a sink or toilet, it can be very dangerous. The dwarf hamster can even get himself killed. To avert any such incident, make sure that the toilet seat is kept down. You can also keep the toilet door closed to make sure that he does not enter the toilet.

You should also make sure that all kind of medicines, syrups and tablets are out of reach of the dwarf hamster. You can also get childproof cabinets in your home to keep all such potentially dangerous stuff in those cabinets.

If there are any areas of the house that the dwarf hamster needs to keep away from, you have to keep them closed and blocked. You should also make sure that the dwarf hamster sleeps in his cage. This is for his safety and also for the good of the family members.

You might also have to use barriers to make sure that the dwarf hamster can't reach certain spots and rooms in the house. But, a point that needs to be noted here is that normal pet barriers can't be used for a dwarf hamster. Even child proofing barriers would not be effective.

This is because your dwarf hamster will happily climb these barriers. He might even get his head stuck in the barrier openings, inviting more trouble for himself and for you also.

You will have to make safe and secure barriers on your own. Or, you could get these barriers from a good pet shop. These barriers should have a very strong base of plastic.

Barriers made of Plexiglas will also serve the purpose right. If you wish to make the barrier at your home, then you can use Plexiglas or wood.

You can also use a good piece of cardboard as a barrier. For example, to keep the dwarf hamster away from the fridge or refrigerator, you can fix the cardboard in the opening. This will prevent the pet from entering the opening. Make sure you use a good quality cardboard.

You can also take some measures to keep the dwarf hamster away from your furniture. This is important so that they don't try to dig by chewing on the fabric. You can fix some heavy material of cardboard at the bottom end of the furniture that you are trying to protect.

This can prevent the pet from digging on the material of the furniture. You can also keep such barriers in front of various rooms. This will make sure that the pet can't enter these rooms. These are simple ways to keep the pet safe and also your things safe.

It is important that you take appropriate steps to proof the home. This will help you to set some limits and boundaries for the pet. These boundaries are for his own good.

There is no use in getting cautious after serious and irrevocable damage has been done. It pays to take all the necessary precautions right from the very beginning.

You will take some time to understand the mannerisms of your pet. It is important to always supervise the pet. If you are unable to do so, you can ask a family member to do so for you. You can use the cage when there is no one around to supervise the pet dwarf hamster.

You can be secure knowing that your pet is safe and sound inside its cage. But, once you understand the pet better, you can take further steps to make sure that things remain safe in the house for the pet. A safe environment is good for everybody in the home.

You can also keep him in the cage when you can't supervise him and his actions. This will allow you to be free and will also ensure that all is fine in the home.

You should make sure that your dwarf hamster plays with the right kind of toys. Cheap plastic materials that can have an adverse effect on the health of the dwarf hamster must be avoided. Similarly, toys that can be shredded or broken should also be avoided.

The dwarf hamster might accidentally swallow the small or shredded pieces. Make sure that the toys that you allow the pet to play with are of good quality. They should be safe for the dwarf hamster, and they should be impossible to swallow for the dwarf hamster.

Your dwarf hamster could actually shock you with the kind of things it can get hurt from. For example, the cardboard rolls of toilet paper can be very harmful for the dwarf hamster because he can get his head stuck in it.

You should make sure any such potentially dangerous things are out of the reach of the dwarf hamster. Keep the waste bin and waste stuff away from him because he might try to play with things that could be harmful for him.

This might be very difficult for you in the beginning to look into areas and places that have hidden dangers for the pet. But, you will definitely learn with time and experience.

The furniture in the house should be dwarf hamster-friendly. You should make sure there are no sharp edges that could hurt the animal. Also, make sure that the dwarf hamster can climb on the furniture.

If you have recliners in your house, keep them away from the pet. The pet could be severely injured by these reclining chairs. If somebody sits on them accidentally while the dwarf hamster is hiding in the spring, the reclining action and the spring could injure the pet.

To be on the safer side, always check the chair or sofa that you are about to sit on. You don't want to sit on your dwarf hamster and injure him.

Your dwarf hamster could climb onto the washing machine and dish washer. So, make sure that these items always have a lid on. To be on the safer side, always check inside the washing machine and the dish washer before operating them.

6. Maintaining hygiene

Hygiene is always an important factor when you are keeping a pet. The pet's surroundings have to be as clean as possible. This is important so that you can keep your pet away from various diseases.

You should also note that it is not enough to buy a pet and provide him with a cage or food. You also have to understand the hygiene requirements of the pet.

Your pet might defecate on the carpet or floor. While you can litter train the pet, you also have to be prepared for such things. An attempt has been made to cover all the necessary issues that you will encounter when planning to take care of the dwarf hamster's hygiene.

You will have to make sure that the cage and the surroundings of the pet are clean. You have to make sure that you have the time or manpower to get the cleaning done.

When you are keeping a dwarf hamster, hygiene is all the more important. You should make sure that you don't fail to meet the standards that are required to keep the pet healthy.

The habitat of the pet should be as clean as possible because a dirty environment will only lead to germs and diseases. Keep the cage clean at all times, without exception.

You have to make sure that your hands are clean before you can feed the dwarf hamster. When the dwarf hamster is sick, you might have to hand feed him. This point becomes all the more important at that time.

Like you would wash your hands after and before eating food, you should maintain a routine of washing your hands nicely with soap before and also after feeding the pet.

These points have been discussed so that you understand the hygiene requirements of your pet. This will help you to understand how you can make sure that your pet is living in a clean environment.

When you are looking to maintain the hygiene for your pet, you should understand that there are certain tasks that you will have to do once a week or once in fifteen days.

There will also be certain cleanliness related tasks that you will have to do every day, such as keeping the litter boxes clean. You can't postpone these tasks to the next day.

You should make sure that these tasks are done on time and that you dedicate yourself to get these tasks done each time. If you fail to do so, the dwarf hamster will have to suffer.

An attempt has been made to cover all the necessary issues that you will encounter when planning to take care of a dwarf hamster. The given points regarding the hygiene of the animal will help you plan keeping the dwarf hamster in a better way.

Everyday tasks:

There are certain tasks that you will have to do on a daily basis. You should make a list of these tasks and should ensure that you or somebody from your place does those tasks every single day.

It is important to clear away the debris on a regular basis. It is also equally important to keep the food and water containers clean. The given list of tasks would need to be done on a daily basis.

The water container of the pet should be cleaned and refilled every day. If there is some water left from the previous day, then make sure that you throw away the water. There should be fresh drinking water for the pet every single day.

There might be faeces in the area where your pet is. You should make sure that the area is cleaned thoroughly every day. There should be no faeces laying around in that area.

It is also important that the food containers of the dwarf hamster are neat and clean. Before you can serve food, make sure that the container is clean. You should throw away any left overs from the previous meal.

You should look for weeds in the enclosure and around the animal. If you let the weeds grow, they can spell disaster for your pet. So, it is important to remove them as soon as possible.

Tasks to be done two or three times a day

There are certain tasks that need to be done at least twice a day. You can fix two days in a week to do these tasks. This will help you to maintain the overall hygiene for your dwarf hamster and his surroundings.

You should also remember to replace the bedding when you think that it is unfit to use now. You should never compromise on the hygiene of your pet.

You should clean the walls of the area that encloses the animal at least once a week. The walls will get dirty and to ensure overall hygiene, you should clean them also.

You should clean the bedding of the animal at least twice a week. This is important because the animal will use that place a lot and automatically it will get dirty. It is important to clean it from time to time.

While you change water every day in the water containers, you should make sure that you scrub the container at least twice a week. The same also goes for food containers.

You should also clean all the twigs and leaves that may be lying in and around the enclosure. The small twigs can hurt the young pets. So, it is important to keep cleaning them from time to time.

Right containers for the food and water

You must be spending a lot of time and energy in deciding the right menu for the dwarf hamster. At the same time, it is also extremely important that you pay importance to the containers that carry its food and water.

While you might wonder about the importance of food containers, you should understand that dirty containers are carriers of allergies and diseases.

These allergies and diseases can further turn into serious problems if not treated well.

So, it is important that you take care from the very beginning and make sure that the right containers are chosen to serve the food items.

You can consider the certain important points to make sure that the food is fed in the right way and in the right containers to the dwarf hamster.

The containers you use should be safe for the animal. You should make sure that they are made from a safe material. Toxic and cheap materials don't last long and also contribute towards the ill-health of the pet.

A poor quality container will make the food spoil. The spoilt food is injurious to the health of your dwarf hamster.

The food and water containers should be sturdy enough to hold all the food and water. The containers should also allow the pet animal to feed himself without any difficulty.

They should also be easy to handle for you. You don't want to spend hours getting the containers right. This will be a waste of your time.

The water container that you choose should allow you to store good quantities of water for a long time. They should not break under the weight.

It is very important that the containers are kept clean. The containers should be washed with good quality soap powder at least two to three times a week. You should also make sure that you remove the left-over food or dirty water from the food and water containers.

7. Tracking a lost dwarf hamster

It is a nightmare for any pet owner to lose a pet. Owing to its small size, it is easy to lose sight of the dwarf hamster. You could lose him very easily. This section will help you to understand what you can do when you lose a dwarf hamster.

A dwarf hamster loves to hide. It can hide for hours. This makes it very important that the pet is monitored all the time. You should allow him to play in areas where you know he will be safe.

It is suggested that you keep food for the pet in brown paper bags around the area where they are hiding. The pet will come out to eat and the noise made by the brown bag will let you know where the pet is.

The best time to search for a dwarf hamster is during the night time. The pet is nocturnal in nature. This allows you a chance to find him roaming around. Remember to carry a flash light with you.

If the pet is not coming out after all these simple tricks, then you have probably lost him. If the pet has escaped outside the home area, then it can be very difficult to get him back.

Another way that is slowly gaining popularity among pet owners is the use of pet collars with chips. This allows you to track the location of the pet on a laptop or other tracking devices.

GPS tracking can help you to locate the dwarf hamster when it is on the run. You can attach the tracking device to the pet's collar and can use the tracking app to know his whereabouts.

8. Neutering or spaying

When you domesticate an animal, it also concerns you to understand its breeding cycles. As an owner, you need to make a decision whether you would want your pets to have progenies or not. This should be a well thought of decision, so that you can take the required actions.

Pet owners have started spaying or neutering their dwarf hamsters now. This practice was not common a few years ago. Even today people don't know as much about it as neutering or spaying of cats and dogs.

The dwarf hamsters can be neutered or spayed by the owners or the breeders. Neutering or spaying has become an important part of dwarf hamster domestication.

When you are sure that you don't want your female pet animal to breed, it is better to spay the animal before it is too late. Similarly, neuter the male dwarf hamster if you don't want breeding. Many breeders sell dwarf hamsters after neutering or spaying the dwarf hamsters.

It should also be understood that neutering or spaying the domestic dwarf hamster will have its consequences on the pet. It is better to understand these consequences, talk to the veterinarian about them and be prepared for them.

The sexual organs of the dwarf hamsters are located towards the inside of the animal are also very small. The entire process can be very tricky and complicated.

It is extremely important that you get the neutering or spaying done by a trained professional who has experience dealing with these exotic pet animals.

9. Vaccination

As a prospective pet owner, it is one of your responsibilities to make sure that the pet's health is not compromised on. One of the easiest ways to do so is to vaccinate the pet on time.

Most pet animals require vaccination against common diseases. They need yearly doses and a booster dose. A dwarf hamster does not require this.

31

You should talk to your veterinarian about the health of the dwarf hamster. At most, the veterinarian might ask you to vaccinate the pet against rabies and distemper.

If your pet eats a lot of insects and meat, you will have to get him treated for parasites. Other than that, there are no annual vaccines that the pet dwarf hamster needs.

10. Legal regulations

When you are studying the pet dwarf hamster, it is important to understand the legal regulations that govern them. This will help you to know how easy it is for you domesticate the dwarf hamster in your country.

If you are looking to bring home a dwarf hamster, then you should contact the animal shelter in your area. You should make sure that you inform yourself well about this and speak to all the concerned and relevant people.

This is important so that you can avert any future issues and problems. You should be sure that the laws permit you to hand raise the animal. This is important because the law prohibits the domestication of certain animals.

This is not just important for the rights of the exotic and wild animals but also the safety of the human beings. So, when you are planning to domesticate the dwarf hamster, you should understand the licensing laws properly.

The dwarf hamster is said to be an animal that belongs to the exotic class. This makes it important to understand the licensing rules before domesticating it. There are certain laws that govern the export, import and domestication of exotic animals.

Make sure that you understand all the laws that govern the domestication of the dwarf hamster. You should understand each detail before you go and bring the dwarf hamster home.

When you are planning to bring an animal home, especially a wild animal or an exotic animal, it is important to understand the licensing rules. If you do something that is against the law, you will have to pay a hefty fine. You would definitely want to save yourself from this trouble.

In case you domesticate an animal against the law, the penalty could even include seizure of the animal. It is better to understand the laws and save the animal from all the unnecessary trouble.

You should make sure that your state makes it legal to own a dwarf hamster because there are a few states that still don't allow the domestication of these exotic animals. You should understand the laws in your state well before you make a final decision.

One of the major concerns of a first time owner of an exotic animal would be to understand the legalities involved in domesticating the animal. It should be noted that exotic animals come under a special category of animals, so it is imperative that the government of each state lays down some clear rules on the domestication of these animals.

If you reside in UK, then the rules that you need to abide by will be different from the rules of US. So, you should take out time to understand the specific rules of your particular state. In the United States, different states have different rules for the domestication of exotic animals.

On the other hand, United Kingdom has rules that are less stringent when compared to the rules of US. Many other countries in Europe also allow domestication of dwarf hamsters. There are rules and regulations for the same, but again they are not very stringent.

United States Licensing

It is known that when looking at the aspect in a legal way, the definition changes between various jurisdictions. This allows each jurisdiction to have some specific laws that govern the hand raising, import and export of the exotic animals.

Each state has its own set of laws. Though the basic structure of the law that governs the keeping of these special animals is similar, the law will change as you move from one state to another.

There are certain states that completely put a ban on the keeping of certain animals. These laws lay emphasis on the idea that the exotic animals are better in the wild, and there is no need to domesticate them.

In some areas, such as Oregon and Idaho, the European dwarf hamsters are considered to be illegal. But on the other hand, the African pygmy is considered legal.

In some places, such as New Jersey and Mainer, you need a legal permit before you can domesticate a dwarf hamster. In places like Virginia, it is illegal to keep dwarf hamsters. You will come under law punishment if you do so.

You should take out enough time to understand the laws and all the ramifications of those laws. These laws also get upgraded from time to time.

This makes it all the more essential to completely understand the current licensing law in your state. The failure to do so will only lead to future complications for you and the animal.

United Kingdom licensing

United Kingdom has its own specific set of laws governing the domestication of exotic animals. In the year 1976, the government had passed a law to keep a check on the domestication of wild and exotic animals.

The law was passed owing to the large number of people who had started hand raising the exotic animals, without realizing how wild and dangerous they can be.

In most places in Europe, the European dwarf hamster is protected. It is illegal to keep it as a domestic pet. The domestication of the African pygmy has less stringent rules.

11. Various costs encountered while domesticating a dwarf hamster

Domesticating an animal is not child's play. While you have to be available emotionally and physically, you also need to provide financial support.

As a prospective owner, you might be wondering the costs that you need to prepare for when buying and then bringing up a dwarf hamster. You will have many doubts in your head.

As the owner and parent of the pet, you will have to make attempts to fulfil all the needs of the animal. You should also be prepared on the financial front to take care of these needs.

It is better that you plan these things well in advance. This planning will help you to avoid any kind of disappointment that you might face when there are some payments that need to be made.

To clear the various doubts in your head, you should understand the nature of the pet and also the various costs that you will incur while raising the pet.

Your pet dwarf hamster will have various things that will make him different from other pets. There will be specific requirements of the pet. For example, in regards to diet and housing, the animal has some very specific needs.

You should be able to understand the needs and then also fulfil them. This section will help you in understanding what you can expect in terms of finances when you are planning to bring a dwarf hamster to your household.

To begin with, you need money to buy the dwarf hamster. Once you have spent money on buying the animal, you should be ready to spend money on his domestication. You can expect to spend money on the shelter, healthcare and food of the animal.

While there are certain purchases that are only one time and fixed, you will also have to be prepared for unexpected purchases that you will have to face once in a while. You have to be ready to bear various other regular things continuously over the years.

Being well prepared is the best way to go about things. There are basically two kinds of costs that you will be looking to incur, which are as follows:

The one-time or initial costs: The initial costs are the ones that you will have to bear in the very beginning of the process of domestication of the animal. This will include the one-time payment that you will give to buy the animal.

The regular or monthly costs: Even when you are done with the one-time payments, there are some other things that you won't be able to avoid. But, these finances can be planned well in advance. You can maintain a journal to keep track of them.

The monthly costs are the ones that you will have to spend each month or once in few months to raise the dwarf hamster. This category includes the costs of the food requirements and health requirements of the pet.

The various regular veterinarian visits, the sudden veterinarian visits and replacement of things come under the monthly category.

The various purchases you can expect

While you are all excited to domesticate the dwarf hamster, you should also start planning for all that you can expect in the future while raising the pet animal. You can expect to incur the following:

Purchase price for dwarf hamster: You can expect to spend $20/£14.78 to $100/£73.91 to purchase your dwarf hamster. The price will depend on the species, colour, age and the health of the animal. The Campbell's dwarf hamster can be purchased at $20/£14.78.

You should make sure that you get the dwarf hamster examined medically before buying it. The examination and tests will also add on to the initial price.

You also have the option to adopt a dwarf hamster. This will help you to avoid the initial purchasing price, though the other costs for raising the animal will remain essentially the same.

If your breeder has taken care of the initial health check-ups, then you should be fine with paying a little extra to this breeder because he has saved you from running here and there to get these important procedures done.

Cage: When you will look for a cage for the dwarf hamster, you will realize that there are great options available for cages in pet shops. You can buy a cage for as low as $50/£37.82 and also as high as $500/£378.25. It clearly depends on your choice and your budget. A decent cage can be expected at $200/£147.25.

The cage is a basic requirement for a pet animal. A pet should be provided with a comfortable cage. The cage should be at least four square feet in its size.

It is always better to get a bigger cage for more comfort of the pet. The floor of the cage should be solid. Also, unsealed wood should be avoided. You can expect to spend $200 on average for the cage of the dwarf hamster.

Bedding for the pet: The bedding for the dwarf hamster is another important purchase. You can either look to buy fabric or particulate bedding.

If you buy liners, you can expect to spend $30/£22.20 to $60/£44.39 once. If you go for paper bedding, you will have to spend $50/£36.99 to $100/£73.99 per year.

Exercise wheel: A dwarf hamster needs to release his energy. If he does not have an exercise wheel, you might find him running in circles in his space. He might also try to use other objects to release his energy.

An exercise wheel is a must have for all dwarf hamsters. These are easily available at all local shops. The absence of an exercise wheel will lead to an increase of weight in the pet, which in turn is the root cause of many health issues in the pet.

It is important that the exercise wheel is at least twelve inches in diameter. This will allow the dwarf hamster to exercise well without injuring himself while running. A smaller wheel might induce back problems in a dwarf hamster.

Depending on the quality of the exercise wheel, you can expect to spend $20/£14.80 to $40/£29.60.

Vet fund: When planning the monthly costs, you can't overlook the cost of visits to the vet. If your dwarf hamster is healthy and fit, even then you should visit the vet at least once a year.

A yearly check-up will help you keep a track on the health and progress of your pet. This yearly visit that would also include some tests should not cost you more than $60/£44.39. This is a cost that you have to pay once a year, but it is better to plan it well ahead of time.

You should also be prepared for unprecedented visits to the vet. If your dwarf hamster falls sick, then you will have to take him to the vet. This is something that you won't be able to plan ahead, but you can set aside a certain amount of money each month for the visits to the doctor.

It is believed that you should have an extra $1000/£776.2 saved for your dwarf hamster's emergencies. He might require an operation or surgery because of a disease.

It is always a good idea to buy insurance so that illness and injuries are covered. You can expect to spend $80/£59.19 per year for the insurance premium.

First aid kit: Though it is always advised to take the pet to the vet if any health problem arises, it is always a great idea to keep a first aid kit ready. This will help in case of minor injuries and also emergencies when you can't reach the vet.

When you keep a first aid kit, it is important that you have knowledge about each item. You should know how to use things. You should also replace stuff when they reach their expiration date.

The various items that the first aid box of the dwarf hamster should have are bottled water, hand warmers, paper towels, flash light, toilet paper, scissors, tweezers, nail clippers, cotton swabs, hydrogen peroxide, saline water, vitamin A cream, vitamin D cream and Neosporin.

You can expect to spend around $50/£36.99 to $60/£44.39 while preparing a basic first aid box for the dwarf hamster.

Litter box: You will have to buy one or more litter boxes for the dwarf hamster. You can also make litter boxes at home. You will need cardboard boxes to make them at home.

You also have to use paper litter shavings to train the pet well for using the litter box. Depending on whether you make the litter box at home or purchase it from the pet store, you can expect to spend $1/£0.74 to $10/£7.40.

There is also probability that the dwarf hamster will not use the litter box. But, it is always better to buy one and train the pet.

Toys and hiding place: As an important accessory for the pet's cage, you will have to invest in good quality toys. You also need to buy a hiding place for the dwarf hamster.

Cheap plastic materials that can have an adverse effect on the health of the dwarf hamster must be avoided. Similarly, toys that can be shredded or broken should also be avoided.

You also need to provide an igloo like structure for your pet to hide in. This will make him feel secure. You can prepare one at home with an old plastic tub or with an inverted cardboard box.

Depending on your choice of toys and hiding place, you can expect to spend about $50/£36.99 to $250/£184.97.

Water and food containers: You will have to buy food and water containers for your pet animal. They will be included in the initial costs. It is important that you invest in good quality containers so that you don't have to buy replacement containers in a few months.

The containers should be bought to suit the animal's requirements. You should plan the number of containers that you would need. You could also think about buying an extra water container.

There are many people who might feel that this is an unnecessary cost, but you should take out time to understand the importance of good food and water containers.

The estimated cost for the food and water container can be $100/£73.99 to $250/£184.97.

Food: The most important factor that will affect your monthly costs is the food of the dwarf hamster. The type of the food and the quality of the food that you give to your pet will make an impact on your monthly expenditure on the pet.

You will have some options when it comes to feeding your dwarf hamster. You can choose amongst those options, depending on the availability of the items in your region and also the price of the food items.

Each kibble pack that has over two pounds of food costs about $10/£7.40 to $30/£22.20.

12. Bringing home a healthy dwarf hamster

A major concern of many prospective owners and buyers of the dwarf hamster is how to make sure that the animal that they are getting home is healthy.

It is extremely critical that you get a healthy pet to your home because once you get an unhealthy animal you will only make things worse for yourself and the pet.

In the excitement of getting a new pet, you shouldn't forget the basic checks that you need to do before bringing the dwarf hamster home. The last thing that anyone would expect after finding a breeder and getting an animal is that it is not in good health.

You will not know how to care for the sick pet. The pet's health will deteriorate. You will be spending thousands of dollars just on the health of the animal.

The following pointers will help you to make sure that your future pet is in the prime of its health:

- Make sure that you learn as much as possible about the dwarf hamster before you decide to buy him and bring him to your home.

- Even if the animal has had health issues in the past, it can be a matter of concern for you.

- It is very important to bring a healthy pet to your home. You should definitely avoid getting an injured animal home.

- First and foremost, you should check the health care card of the animal that you wish to buy. All good breeders will maintain a health card, which will have all the details of past diseases and infections. This health card will also help you to understand the vaccines cycle of the animal.

- You should check the health card of the dwarf hamster. If there is an occurrence of genetic disorders in the previous generation of the dwarf hamster, you should avoid buying him because these can't be treated.

- A younger dwarf hamster will have issues that could be different from an older dwarf hamster. You need to make sure that you understand all these issues in detail. If you are buying an older dwarf hamster, you need to be all the more vigilant because they could carry some infections.

- It is important that you closely examine your prospective pet. You should look for any abrasions on his skin. His skin should not be torn or bruised anywhere.

- You should make it a point to check the body temperature of the dwarf hamster. The body temperature should be normal. If the pet is too cold or too hot to touch, then there is some problem with its health.

- You should closely look for any kind of injuries. If you find anything that does not seem normal, then you need to discuss it with the breeder.

- The dwarf hamster should not have any broken limbs. You should be able to check this manually. You should look for any hanging limbs. A hanging head or limb could mean that the pet is severely injured.

- Also, carefully inspect the stomach area. There should be no abrasions.

- It is important that the dwarf hamster is devoid of any infections or diseases when you bring him home.

- It is advisable to take the help of a qualified veterinarian to be sure of the animal's health conditions. He will be the best judge of his condition. A good vet will always guide you in the right direction for the dwarf hamster.

- You should discuss at length about the concerns that you have regarding the pet. You should follow all the instructions that the doctor gives you because they will be for the benefit of the animal.

- You should only keep the pet animal if you are convinced that you will be able to care for the little animal.

- After you have brought the dwarf hamster home, you should keep him isolated for a few days to keep an eye on him. You should allow him inside the house only after a few days of checking if everything is normal with the dwarf hamster. In case of any issues, you should consult the veterinarian or the breeder.

Chapter 3: Understanding the behaviour of a Russian dwarf hamster

There is a lot of controversy on various topics related to dwarf hamsters and dwarf hamster care. This makes it all the more important for a first time owner to do his research right.

You should try to understand all aspects of dwarf hamster care in great detail. Ask more questions, and read about experiences of other pet parents. This will help you a lot in the long run.

It is also important to understand that there is a difference between the easiest way and the best way. You should try to choose the best possible way to do things for your dwarf hamster and not just the easiest way.

Once you have decided that you want to domesticate a dwarf hamster, you will have to prepare for the next step of bringing the pet to your home and helping him to adjust.

This chapter will help you to prepare for this step in the best possible way. It should be fine to spend some extra money if you are able to ensure a better life for the pet dwarf hamster.

As the pet parent, you have to make sure that you understand the behaviour of your pet. You can assume that your pet will behave like other animals.

If you are looking forward to domesticate a dwarf hamster then you should understand that this animal is very different from other usual pets. It is important to understand the behaviour and temperament of the specific animal that you wish to domesticate.

This will help you to be a better master. Your pet might still have some surprises for you, but it is better to know of the general behaviour of the animal.

A dwarf hamster is generally a prey in the wild. Because of this the animal is very defensive in nature. It will get frightened easily. He will get stressed and will not be the first one to attack.

You will be surprised to know that the dwarf hamster is very good in hiding sickness and illness. If you are not careful, you will miss the symptoms which can worsen the condition of a sick pet.

A dwarf hamster will also make a lot of noises. A dwarf hamster makes noises even when he is sleeping.

1. Interpreting the various actions of the dwarf hamster

You should also understand the various actions that your dwarf hamster is likely to do. You should also understand the usual meanings of these actions.

- **Curling in a ball**: They might curl or roll into a ball if they are afraid. They might be in a discomfort or might distrust the other person of animal.

- **Biting**: While some dwarf hamsters can bite out of habit, most others bite because they are angry or afraid. They can also bite if they are attracted by some smell.

- **Splatting**: Splatting is an action when the pet stretches out his legs and rests on the belly. This is done when he is very comfortable. It can also be done when he is too warm.

- **Shaking**: A dwarf hamster might shake and hiss when he is very sad or upset.

- **Anointing**: They will do this when they are around someone or something with a very strong scent or smell.

Biting

If your dwarf hamster gets into a habit of biting, it is important to understand the reasons behind the biting. This will help you to remove the problem.

Most dwarf hamsters do not have a habit to bite unnecessarily. There will always be some trigger that will lead the dwarf hamster to such behaviour.

If your pet has been biting lately, you will have to deal with this problem with a lot of patience. You don't want to give him the wrong signal. This can make things very difficult for the both of you.

Some owners think that cage is the answer to all problems. You shouldn't force the pet to get into the cage each time he bites. He might start associating loneliness to biting.

He might just start biting you each time he wants to be left all alone. There are better ways to deal with this problem. The best way is to try various solutions and see what works for your pet.

Give the pet some food. If the pet is hungry, he will eat the food. This might alter his behaviour. If you feel that the new cream or perfume that you are wearing could be behind the biting then stop wearing it.

It is best to keep a certain kind of soap which you should use to wash your hands each time you approach your pet. In times of confusion, it is always best to use unscented soap solutions.

If the pet tries to hold on to your clothes while biting, don't push him in anger. This will hurt him badly. In addition to the physical injury, the pet will be traumatised. Even you can get injury in this process.

The pet might start avoiding out if you fail to handle him gently. Just sit quietly of he is trying to hold on to something. He will let go off you in some time.

Another trick is to blow some air from your mouth on the dwarf hamster. This will encourage him to leave you. Be gentle so that the pet is not startled or hurt.

If he is trying to reach out to a certain body part, you should make sure that the body part is out of reach of the pet. For example, if he reaches for your hand, use a blanket to hold him for a few days.

Anointing

Another behaviour that the pet dwarf hamster might display is anointing. There is also a chance that the pet never does it.

It is known that anointing is totally related to the sense of smell of the pet dwarf hamster. He will display this behaviour when his olfactory nerves are charged and triggered in some way.

Anointing is when the animal releases a lot of froth from his mouth. This can scare any new pet parent. But, this is normal and you should not get scared.

It is also known as anting or self-anointing. The pet will take various shapes and forms while he is anting. This is also normal and there is nothing to worry about.

The main reason as to why the pet dwarf hamster anoints is still unknown. Many dwarf hamster lovers believe that the animal does so to scare off bigger animals and predators in the wild.

The pet gets very involved when it is anointing. There are many who consider this an apt opportunity to trim the nails of the pet dwarf hamster. But, you need to be very careful so that you don't hurt the pet.

The problem starts when the pet releases froth on you or your clothes. This behaviour should not be encouraged. You should leave the pet alone when it is in an anointing phase.

A smell that the pet likes might trigger the senses of the pet. For example, if you put on a cream that the pet seems to like a lot, he might display this behaviour.

2. Noises made by the dwarf hamster

While you will learn about all the unique traits that your pet dwarf hamster has by experiencing him and spending time with him, there are some traits that almost all the members of his species will exhibit.

It is beneficial to know of these traits so that you are not taken off guard. You will be able to understand what is normal for this animal and what is not. This will help you to be more prepared and not be confused every time something happens.

A dwarf hamster is known to make certain kinds of noises. These noises can scare a pet owner, but you should know that most of these noises are nothing but normal behaviour.

He is a noisy pet and it is in the basic nature of the animal to be loud and extremely noisy. This trait of the animal will also affect your decision to domesticate him. This will be a difficult decision for you because your dwarf hamster will not stop making noises.

You should understand the reasons behind these noises. The noises that the dwarf hamster makes are a way of expressing something that he feels. If you understand this natural behaviour of the dwarf hamster, it will be easier for you to deal with them.

Various studies have also suggested that these animals use different kinds of noises to communicate. They make use of various kinds of sounds depending on the situation they are in.

You can expect your pet dwarf hamster to make noises even in the night time. You have to make arrangements so that the noises made by the dwarf hamster don't disturb your family and kids.

The dwarf hamsters can make many different kinds of noises. This section will help you to understand the kinds of noises the dwarf hamster is capable of making and the inherent meaning of the noise.

- **Screaming**: When the dwarf hamster is frightened for his life, he will make loud noises. You should never take such sounds lightly. You need to investigate to understand what has happened. You should observe your pet to understand what is wrong with him.

- **Squealing**: This signifies that the pet dwarf hamster is very terrified or upset or is in pain. He would also make this noise when he is sick or infected by some bacteria or virus.

- **Chirping**: Chirping is the sound made by the dwarf hamster when it is looking for attention. It could want your attention or could be showing interest in another dwarf hamster. The animal could also be hungry when he makes this sound.

- **Snuffling**: Snuffling is also referred to as wheeling. This when the dwarf hamster is in curious mood. The dwarf hamster will go around sniffing things in an attempt to explore more. The animal will follow a particular scent and will also wiggle its little nose.

- **Purring**: This is the sound of happiness. Like most other animals, the dwarf hamster purrs when it is happy and satisfied. When he purrs, you can be sure that he is having a good time.

- **Clicking**: This signifies that the pet dwarf hamster is very scared.

- **Hissing**: When the dwarf hamster is frightened or angry, it will make noises that sound like a hiss. This is known as hissing. You have to closely observe your pet to understand what is wrong with him.

3. Tips to help the dwarf hamster adjust

Once you have brought the pet home, you have to help him adjust to the new surroundings. You should make the entire process gradual so that it is simpler for the dwarf hamster.

The pet can get stressed very easily, which will further make the transitioning more difficult. You should start focusing on bonding with your pet so that he does not get all flustered and stressed.

It is suggested that a routine be followed. Take out some time every day and spend it with the dwarf hamster. The dwarf hamster will use your scent to get used to you.

Follow some tasks every single day and you will notice the pet getting comfortable with you. For example, take him in your arms and pet it, be around him when he plays in the pen and allowing him to sleep on your lap on his dwarf hamster bag.

Don't worry if the pet is a little reserved initially. He will slowly get used to your scent and will associate it with security. This will help the two of you to bond well.

Don't make things difficult for him by introducing him to many people at the same time. This will overwhelm him and stress him out. Make sure that he is not introduced to too many new sounds and smells.

Do it slowly and allow him time to understand these new things and get used to them.

When you are holding the dwarf hamster, try to sit on the floor. If the pet suddenly leaps out of your hold, he won't hurt himself by falling on the ground.

You might also be scared about how you will handle the dwarf hamster. You can use bare hands to hold him. But, if you are not comfortable with his fur, it is suggested that you use a blanket.

You can use a small blanket to hold him comfortably. You can also go for dwarf hamster bags that are easily available.

4. Bonding with the pet

When you domesticate an animal, one of your main concerns will be that you should be able to bond well with the pet. The last thing you want is the pet avoiding any interaction with you.

This section will help you to understand some simple ways to bond well with your dwarf hamster.

A dwarf hamster will always identify people by their smell. You should keep a worn shirt in the cage near the bedding of the pet. This will give him a chance to get used to your scent.

Make sure that the cloth that you choose is a simple one. It should not have loose threads and beads that can harm the pet. Your pet will be fond of simple routine.

It is not a good idea to plan surprises for him. Don't surprise him with new things. Let him get comfortable with things.

You should try to prepare a schedule for everything, such as what time you will feed him, what time you will play with him and what time will you switch on and off the lights.

Preparing a simple schedule and following it each day prepares the dwarf hamster. He starts understanding what he should be expecting. He will slowly start getting more and more comfortable with you this way.

When you play with him each day, try to wash your hands with the same soap solution. This will also help him identify you. These are simple ways to make him get comfortable with you.

If your pet is being difficult, don't be harsh and rude. The pet will get scared and all the hard work that you did will be in vain. If he is not coming out of his blanket, give him some time. Don't force him.

You should also try to keep the pet close to you when you are busy doing other things. For example, while you are watching television, gently hold the pet and keep him in your lap.

Simple acts like these will help the pet dwarf hamster realize that he can be comfortable in your pet and just sleep away without any worry.

The way you hold the pet will also decide how well the pet associates with you. When you want to hold the pet, bring both your hands towards the pet from the two sides.

Place your hands under his belly and lift him gently. Your grip should be firm but not too tight. You should give the pet some room to adjust himself. He should be comfortable in your hold.

5. Things to avoid

There are a few things that you should always try to avoid if you wish to bond well with your pet. This section will help you to understand what you should not do when you are trying to bond well with the pet.

Never wear gloves when you are with the dwarf hamster. The pet will relate to your smell. If you wear gloves, the pet will not be able to do so. The dwarf hamster will repel the gloves because of the weird smell.

This might agitate the pet to a level that he might start biting. If you need to use something, use a clean blanket. But, try to use your bare hands most of the times.

You should be careful of the times that you choose to interact with your pet. If you have had a meal, you might smell of the food that you have consumed.

The strong smells might repel the pet and he might get irritated. If you have played with or touched some other animal, you should stay away from your dwarf hamster for a while because this will also irritate him.

You should never mix up smells because this will confuse the pet animal. If you smell of some food or some other animal, make sure you wear off the smell before your dwarf hamster comes near you.

You should always remember that the dwarf hamster associates with you because of your scent. That scent makes him feel safe and secure. If that is gone, he will get insecure.

Dwarf hamsters are very sensitive to various kinds of noises. You should never make the mistake of talking too loudly in front of them.

You should also avoid loud noises, such as loud music and television. Loud sounds can irritate them.

6. Breeding in Russian dwarf hamsters

A female dwarf hamster will get sexually matured by the age of about four months. If you are interested in breeding your dwarf hamsters then this section will help you to understand the procedure. But, you should understand that breeding in dwarf hamsters has its own challenges.

This section will help you to understand the mating patterns of your pet. The male and female dwarf hamsters have different mating patterns. This will help you to understand the dwarf hamsters in a better light.

You should only breed your dwarf hamsters if you are a serious breeder. Breeding just for fun or to gift baby dwarf hamsters to your friends is not recommended. This is because breeding can be very tricky and life threatening if gone wrong.

In fact, it is widely known that each time dwarf hamsters are bred there is a serious threat to the female dwarf hamster. You should keep this in mind before you attempt breeding of the dwarf hamster.

Breeding is defined as the production of an offspring by mating by the animals. How well you understand the mating patterns of your pet dwarf hamsters will also determine how well you look after the pet.

The time required for a male dwarf hamster to get sexually mature is slightly different from the time required by the female dwarf hamster.

A male and a female dwarf hamster are sexually mature by the time they are seven weeks of age. But, it is highly recommended not to breed the dwarf hamsters at such a young age. It is not healthy for both of them.

It is important that a female dwarf hamster is bred before she is one year old. If your female dwarf hamster is more than a year old and has not been bred, then it is better not to breed her. It can be injurious to her health.

The female of all dwarf hamster species needs to be at least three months of age. So, the best time to breed a female dwarf hamster for the first time is between six months of age to one year. The male should be about three to four months of age. This is the ideal time to breed.

The breeding of dwarf hamsters is often said to be challenging. The reason behind this is that because these animals have a pattern that is different from commonly domesticated animals, it becomes challenging and tricky.

This makes it difficult for people to observe and then understand their breeding and mating routines. It is better to understand as much as you can before going for the process of breeding.

It is known that the males play an active part in the mating process. The females might remain extremely timid and passive during the entire process of mating. The male is known to be focussed and concentrated towards the act from the start to the end.

Dwarf hamsters don't take much time to complete the entire process. There is no need for extra play time. It is known that the breeding will be over in a matter of minutes.

The owner should not keep the male and female together for long periods. If this is done, the male dwarf hamster will try to mate with the female all the time, which is not ideal for her. She can fall sick and can also risk her life.

The male also needs to be away from the babies. There have been reported incidents where the dwarf hamster ate his own young ones right after they were born. You would definitely want to avoid such incidents.

Gestation is defined as development of the child inside the womb of the mother. The gestation period is the time from the conception to the time of the birth of the child. This is the time required by the baby to develop inside the mother's womb.

It is known that the gestation period is usually for about eighteen to twenty five days. It can extend up to thirty five days in some dwarf hamsters.

A female dwarf hamster who is about to give birth to young ones should not be disturbed much. You should provide her with food and water on time, but not be too intrusive in the space of the female dwarf hamster.

You will know that the female has given birth when there are sounds similar to squeaking from the cage. Don't make the mistake of cleaning the cage at this time. Let things be the way they are.

It is advised to clean the cage only after the young ones are at least four weeks of age. This is the time when the babies will slowly start eating from the food that is kept for the mother.

Another important period in the development of the baby is the nursing time. The process of weaning should happen when the young ones are about six weeks of age. The young ones are called pups. The entire group of pups born at a time is referred to as a litter.

Hand raising an infant

The mother dwarf hamster can reject one or more of her babies. This is a very common phenomenon. If the mother decides to reject one or more of the pups, you will have to hand-raise them. It can be very overwhelming for any pet-parent.

You will have to be patient with your pet infant. This is the key. Try to understand the position of a new born and never force him to do anything. Just try to give him a warm and secure environment. This is very important.

If you are hand raising an infant, there are many precautions that you will have to take. The initial phase of trying to nurse the baby can be stressful and challenging for you. But slowly as the days progress, things will get easier.

You will have to make sure that you feed the baby once every three hours. This is a must no matter what time of the day it is. It is essential that you follow this schedule till the infant is at least four weeks of age.

The infant requires less quantities of milk at regular intervals. You can use an eye dropper to feed the infant. You can also use syringes. You can also make use of special plastic bottles that you can squeeze to put small quantities of milk in the dwarf hamster's mouth.

You should avoid giving cow's milk to the infant. Dwarf hamsters, be it adults or young ones can't digest cow's milk well. You could feed him sheep's milk.

You can mix one raw egg in sheep's milk to prepare a healthy formula for the baby dwarf hamster. After the dwarf hamster is about three weeks old, you can mix banana to add fibre to the mixture.

You can also use goat's milk as it is also healthy for the dwarf hamster's development. If you are using raw eggs, remember not to put too many in. A small amount is sufficient for the young dwarf hamster.

It might take some time, but the dwarf hamster will become a little settled with time. You will see him being more comfortable and less restless. The baby should be enjoying a constant warm temperature.

Before you can start feeding your infant, wrap the infant safely in a blanket. After doing this, you can put a heating pad over the blanket. This will help to keep the infant warm. You will have to constantly monitor the heating pad so that it does not over heat the infant.

You should keep the infant close to you as much as possible. Your body warmth is also important for the infant to feel safe. When you are feeding him with the bottle, try to keep the blanket carrying him close to your body in your lap.

When you try to feed the infant, he might resist the feed or might just reject using the bottle or syringe for drinking the milk. This is a normal behaviour by the animal and you should patiently keep trying.

Don't force him. Just gently keep trying and finally the infant will take to the milk formula and also the bottle feeding.

You can try opening the mouth of the infant with the help of your index finger and thumb. Make sure that you are as gentle and soft as possible. You can also close his eyes with your hand when you are trying to feed him. These are simple tricks that can help you to feed a baby that is not being very cooperative.

You can easily find commercially available milk formulas, which are high in the minerals that the infant needs. You can purchase these milk formulas from a shop that stocks stuff related to dwarf hamsters.

You should make sure that the water you use to prepare the formula has been cooled after heating it. It should be noted that you should not use cold water because it is not right for the formula.

You should also not use boiling water because it can again destroy the mineral content of the formula. A simple way to make use of the water is to boil the water, and then let the boiled water cool down.

You can also look for them online, where they are easily available. These packs come with printed instructions. You can easily follow the instructions and give your baby dwarf hamster the healthiest drink.

Once you have prepared a formula for the baby dwarf hamster, you should remember never to heat it again. This can destroy the mineral consistency in the formula.

If you have prepared extra than what you need immediately then you can safely store the formula in the refrigerator.

It has been noticed with the infants that they might take some time to get used to you and the new surroundings. The nursing time will also become easier and also memorable after they are more comfortable in the surroundings and with you.

If your infant is rejecting the milk or the milk formula that is being served to him, then there could be another reason than him being uncomfortable in the new surroundings.

Try to keep him warm. Give him some time to adjust to the new surroundings. If the problem still persists, it is important that you consult the veterinarian about this. He will be able to help you in this case.

While you are feeding the baby, you should be very particular about the hygiene of the baby and his surroundings. If there is any milk spillage, clean it immediately so that the area does not become a breeding place for diseases and infections.

Another point that you need to remember is that the infant's bottles need to be cleaned after they are used. Some people don't wash it every time it is used. This is not right. You need to clean it every single time it is used.

Chapter 4: Housing and Husbandry

Your pet dwarf hamster will not adapt too well to changing surroundings. You will have to make sure that you provide the animal with everything that he needs to live a good life.

This chapter is an attempt to help you understand the importance of a shelter or a cage in an animal's life. You will be able to understand the basic concerns while building the cage for the dwarf hamster.

When you are setting up a cage for the dwarf hamster, you need to make sure that the cage is set up in a way that is inviting for the pet. The animal should not feel captive or like a prisoner in the cage. If the pet animal is not comfortable, he will begin to get stressed, which is something that you wouldn't want.

The cage should be built keeping in mind the basic nature of the pet. You can't build a cage that is suitable for a dog or a cat. You have a dwarf hamster and your cage should be built keeping in mind his natural behaviour, instincts, likes and dislikes. This is the best for you and also for the animal.

Like you need a home, an animal also needs a place and space that he can call his home. A home should make him happy and should be inviting for him. When the home does not provide the comfort and security that it should, it can lead to detrimental results.

While it is important to have a cage, it is also important that the cage is of the right size. The advisable dimensions and specifications of the cage have also been listed. This will help you to build or a get a cage that is most suitable for your pet.

There are many owners who might feel that there is no need to set up a cage because the pet can stay indoors. But, you need to remember that even if you are a hands-on parent of the pet, there will be times when the pet would be unsupervised.

There will be times when you will have to concentrate on some other work and the dwarf hamster would be alone. The cage is very handy at such times because you can do your work and can also be sure that your pet is safe and sound in the cage that you have built for him.

Also, during the night time, it is best for the pet and also for the family members that the pet is in his cage. The pet will get used to the cage and your family members can also sleep without any tensions of your pet being loose in the house.

You should understand that just because the dwarf hamster is a small animal does not mean that you can keep it anywhere. You need a proper cage for him. You should never keep him in a glass environment such as an aquarium. Such places don't allow the flow of air and can cause breathing issues in the pet.

It is important to have the right temperature for the animal. If the temperature is more or less than the ideal temperatures, it can be fatal for the pet. You can keep the pet inside the house in controlled temperatures. Nothing is more important than the health and well-being of the pet.

When you look for a cage for the dwarf hamster, you will realize that there are great options available for cages in pet shops. You can buy a cage for as low as $50/£37.82 and also as high as $500/£378.25. It clearly depends on your choice and your budget.

This chapter will help you to understand what you need to do to make sure that the surroundings of the pet dwarf hamster are exactly the way he requires it.

1. The right bedding for the dwarf hamster

It is also important that the right kind of bedding is provided for the dwarf hamster. This is a simple way of keeping the pet animal comfortable and stress free.

The bedding needs to be comfortable for the pet. It should also be cost effective for you. You will have many choices when you go out to buy bedding. This section will help you understand what you should choose and why.

The bedding that you choose for the dwarf hamster should be safe, easy to clean and easy to change. It should allow the pet to roam around also. You can get the right bedding for your pet from a pet store that sells dwarf hamster products.

The following are the different kinds of bedding that you can consider:

Liners

There are cage liners easily available on the market. You can use these to line the bottom of the cage. They are easy to attach and detach, so are very popular amongst owners.

It is also important that the cage is deep for this type of setting. The liners should be made from a good quality fabric. These liners are safe for the pet because they don't have sharp pieces that can hurt him.

It is easier for the dwarf hamster to walk on these liners. Fabric liners are actually considered as the best option for a dwarf hamster's cage.

One disadvantage of these liners would be that the pet will try to dig into them and might also spill his food and water. It can be inconvenient for the pet-parent at such a time.

Wood shavings

Another popular choice of bedding for the cage is wood shavings. It is important that the shavings are free from phenol. It is also important that the cage is deep otherwise the shavings will just fall off.

The pet can safely dig in these wood shavings. It is easier to do so for him. He can have his fun in this simple way. The wood shavings are relatively odourless because they allow air amongst the shavings.

The wood shavings also have some disadvantages. The shavings will keep falling in the eye of the pet. They might fall in the water or food container. This can be unhealthy for the pet dwarf hamster.

You can use aspen shavings. They are considered the safest of all. The second choice of shavings could be kiln dried pine shavings.

You should not use untreated pine shavings or cedar shavings. These can be harmful for the pet.

Paper bedding

If you can't install liners in the cage of the dwarf hamster, then this is your second best option. They look quite similar to the wood shavings.

One downside of this kind of bedding is that the paper bedding is very dusty in nature. This might lead to dry skin in your dwarf hamster. If your pet already had dry skin, the condition might be aggravated.

The pet can safely dig in these shavings. It is easier to do so for him. He can have his fun in this simple way. The dwarf hamster might also try to chew this kind of bedding. This can be very dangerous and needs to be discouraged.

2. Building the right cage

It was considered amongst the dwarf hamster community that a minimum of two square feet floor size is sufficient for the dwarf hamster. But with increasing awareness, this has changed.

If you wish the dwarf hamster to exercise on the exercise wheel and also have some space to move around, you need a minimum of four square feet floor size. If you can afford a size of six feet or above, it is ideal for the pet.

The feet of the dwarf hamster are meant only to walk on solid surfaces. This should be kept in mind when designing the floor of the cage. You have to avoid wire mesh for the floor of the cage.

It should also be noted that nothing inside the cage should smell too strong. This can affect the respiratory system of the animal. The stuff inside the cage should also not absorb the urine of the pet dwarf hamster.

You should make sure that the sides of the cage do not have wide spaces. The dwarf hamster might just escape from those spaces. You should cover these spaces if there are any.

The cage should also provide proper ventilation. The door should be big enough to let you remove the exercise wheel and other things while cleaning the cage.

It is important that the bedding of the pet is soft and comfortable so that he can slide in and feel comfortable. But, make sure that you check the bedding every day to know whether the pet dwarf hamster has been chewing on its material.

This can be dangerous so you need to replace such items. If the dwarf hamster does not get what it wants, the pet will get stressed and might withdraw from you. The type of cage that you choose for the animal will directly affect the physical health and mental health of your pet dwarf hamster.

When you are building a cage for the dwarf hamster, you have to make sure that you have provisions for the most basic and important things, such as food and water. The ideal cage will be spacious enough. It will allow the animal to roam around freely and rest well when it wants to.

You can use two big containers for food and water. It is important that the pet has access to food and water at all times. You don't want to be busy somewhere else when your pet is stressed with the lack of water.

The best buy for a cage is the one that can be cleaned easily. The cage should be comfortable and fun for the pet, but also easy to clean for you. You can go for a cage with liners on the floor.

Such bottoms can be lifted for cleaning purposes. But, make sure that the liner fabric can't be chewed by the pet dwarf hamster. You can also go for the metal bottomed cage, but you need to be extra careful with these kinds of cages.

You will have to make sure that such cages are not exposed to faeces and urine, otherwise they will rust. You can buy mats and rugs that can be thrown after use to cover such bottoms.

You should be careful in choosing the material of the floor. You don't want to choose a fabric that secretes oils. These oils can cause damage to the liver of the animal and can also affect his respiratory system.

You should also keep the litter box and the food and water containers on opposite sides. The pet should not be encouraged to defecate in a place where he eats food.

You will have to take certain precautions with the litter box also. The pet will try to dig in a very clean litter box. To avoid this issue, you should be keeping paper litter in the box.

You can easily get paper litter that is recyclable. Also, make sure that this is shredded or in pellet form. If you get the clumping or the clay litter, these can get stuck in the nasal passage of the dwarf hamster when they try to smell the box.

While getting the cage, you should remember that a certain amount of privacy is needed by the pet. This is important so that the dwarf hamster can be healthy at a mental level.

If you are planning to domesticate more than one dwarf hamster, you can consider buying another cage. This cage could be very simple and basic. This will allow space for the dwarf hamsters.

The extra cage will also help you to isolate the sick dwarf hamster. A vet will always advise you to isolate a sick pet. This is necessary so that the pet can recuperate nicely in the absence of other pets.

He would need some space to himself. What is also important is that he does not transmit the disease to the healthy pets. The isolation helps to avoid such a situation also.

You can either build your own cage, or can buy commercial cages. Just because the dwarf hamster is a small animal does not mean that you can keep it anywhere.

If you are looking for a financially viable option, then you can buy an already used cage. You can use plastic cages that are custom made for guinea pigs and rabbits. You can also use cages made for chinchillas.

3. Accessories

One of the safest ways to welcome a new pet is to provide him with a good shelter. The shelter should be as comfortable as possible. While you might save money from buying a cheap cage, you need to understand what is important.

When you bring a pet home, the pet will be scared of the new surroundings. You will have to make all the attempts that will help the pet to adjust in the new environment.

When you are planning the furnishing and accessories of the shelter, then you should make sure that you give the pet an environment that closely resembles his natural habitat. This will keep him happy and spirited.

And when the pet is happy, then everything is great. Besides the basic stuff, such as food and water, it is also important to accessorize the cage well.

This is important because the right accessories will help him to feel like he is at home. They will bring him closer to his natural habitat and natural tendencies.

Dwarf hamsters love to dig. A simple way to keep the dwarf hamster happy is to give him an old t-shirt or piece of cloth. The animal will love it. He will act as if he is digging in the t-shirt.

He will also try to fit in the t-shirt. This will keep him busy and happy. This will become one of his favourite things to play with. Your smell on the t-shirt will also help him to bond with you better.

There are several accessories available these days that will help you to keep your dwarf hamster happy. If you go to a pet shop, you will get many ideas for the accessories that you can keep in the cage of the pet.

There are many types of bedding available these days that can help your dwarf hamster to have rest and also fun when he wants. For example, you can get bedding in the shape of a cave. This will be fun for the pet dwarf hamster.

You can also buy some simple stuffed toys for the pet animal. The right kind of toys should be bought for the dwarf hamster. It is important that the toys are made of a good quality material.

They should not be harmful for the pet. Your dwarf hamster will take them in his mouth, so they should be of a good quality. It is better if the toys are washable. This will enable you to wash the dwarf hamster's toys every now and then when they are dirty.

4. Cleaning the cage

The pet can't clean the cage on its own, and if it is forced to stay in an unhygienic environment, he will fall sick.

It is extremely important to clean the cage of the pet. You will not necessarily enjoy this process, but still you have to do it.

Once a week, you should clean the entire cage. You should thoroughly clean it with a clean cloth. Remember that the dwarf hamster should not be in the cage when the cleaning procedure is going on.

There are certain tasks that you need to do daily, while several others need to be done once a week. If the bedding is soiled, it should be cleaned on a daily basis.

While you are busy cleaning the cage of the pet dwarf hamster, it is important that you check the cage thoroughly. If the pet has littered in an area other than the litter box, then it should be cleared and disinfected properly. You should make it a point to do this check on a daily basis.

You can keep baby wipes handy to clean something immediately. It is important that the cage is free from all bacteria and viruses that are known to cause diseases in pet animals. You should keep some time designated for the cleaning of the cage.

The litter box needs to be disinfected once a week. The toys of the dwarf hamster should be washed once every two weeks, if the toys are washable.

Similarly, if the food and water containers look dirty, they should be cleaned and refilled.

The litter box needs to be cleared every day. The litter box and the floor of the cage can be cleaned with the help of a mixture of bleach and water. The mixture should have 98 percent water and only two percent bleach.

This daily and weekly cleaning procedure is important so that the surroundings of the dwarf hamster remain healthy. The bacteria in the dust and dirt can harm the pet animal.

If you are using bleach to clean the litter box, then you should make sure that there are no residues on the box. The dwarf hamster can try to lick any residue that he may find on the box or the cage. Bleach can be very harmful and dangerous to the pet animal.

You should not use very strong disinfectants. Such products can be very harmful if they ingested even in the smallest of quantities. You should always look for mild anti-bacterial soaps and detergents to clean the vessels and the floor.

A simple procedure that you can follow once every week to clean the cage thoroughly is to fill a bucket with clean water. Pour in some anti-bacterial detergent that you wish to use. Form a nice lather in the bucket. This can be used to clean the toys and the containers. The remaining can be used to clean the floor nicely.

After you have cleaned the floor with the detergent, use plain water to wash off any sign of the detergent. This will ensure that the dwarf hamster does not ingest anything harmful.

It is also very important that you let the floor dry completely before you allow the dwarf hamster to come inside the cage. He could spoil the floor and could create a mess for you to clean again. He could even try to drink any residue that he finds on the floor. To avoid all these hassles, you should allow the floor to dry completely.

Avoid using scented soaps and cleaners. Because the dwarf hamster has a strong sense of smell, there is a chance that he gets irritated by the scent of the cleaner.

If you are using liners for the cage of the pet dwarf hamster, then it is also important to change these liners on a regular basis. You can change them once in every two weeks.

Chapter 5: Diet Requirements of the dwarf hamster

The diet of the dwarf hamster will have a direct effect on the way he feels and functions. You should make sure that the staple diet of the pet is able to provide him with all the necessary nutrients.

The dwarf hamster will also enjoy the treats that you serve him. Maintain a good balance between the staple items and treats. You can choose from various food items, such as vegetables, fruits, insects, eggs and meat to provide wholesome nutrition to the pet.

The pet dwarf hamster is a hybrid between the African dwarf hamster species. These hybrids are not found in the wild, and would not be able to survive well. So, it is better not to replicate the diet of a wild dwarf hamster.

You can expect him to acquire deficiencies and diseases when he is not fed good quality food. The cure this is taking the pet to the veterinarian. This in turn will only cost you more money.

Keep the pet healthy by feeding him with high quality foods, rather than spending money on him by taking him to the veterinarian.

1. The nutritional requirement of the dwarf hamster

People still don't know much about the nutritional requirements of the dwarf hamster. There are lot of studies and research that are still being done to understand the nutritional requirements of the dwarf hamster.

You should try to provide certain staples in the everyday food of the dwarf hamster. These staples are insects, fruits, vegetables, eggs and meat. You should also make sure that the food that you choose to serve is of a good quality.

The owners have the choice of feeding cat food or dog food to the pet dwarf hamster. It is important to check all the ingredients of commercial foods to be sure that the food is safe for the dwarf hamster.

You should never go by the brand picture to buy your pet's food. It is important to check the main ingredients and percentage of each ingredient.

It is better if the main ingredient of these foods is meat. You should avoid any food that has by-products of animals instead of the real food. You should also avoid food with ingredients such as BHT, BHA and ethoxyquin.

A pet dwarf hamster is usually served kibble as its main food. Kibble is a nutritious meal that is ground into bite sized pellets for the pets.

When you are buying kibble, you should also look for the ideal size. The dwarf hamster might not be able to eat a bigger size, and might even choke in it.

You can look for X shaped and Y shaped kibble for the pet because they are easier to eat and swallow.

You should also make sure that the percentage content of each nutrient is just right for the dwarf hamster. It has been discovered that too much protein in the diet of the pet can lead to kidney problems.

The percentage of fat in the diet of the pet dwarf hamster will depend on the individual needs of your pet. If your pet dwarf hamster is gaining weight, you might want to lower the fat in his diet.

If you are looking to feed your pet dwarf hamster a simple yet good diet then you can go for cat food along with some occasional insects. These insects will provide the necessary fibre in the diet of the pet.

Dog food is also considered to be highly nutritious for the pet dwarf hamster. It is believed that it is better than the cat food, but the food pieces are bigger, which can be difficult for the pet dwarf hamster to chew.

An ideal pet dwarf hamster diet would consist of up 25 - 30 percent of protein, 10 – 15 percent of fat, 40 percent of carbohydrates, 10 - 15 percent of fibre and minimum of 2 percent of vitamins and minerals.

The protein in the diet can be primarily given by mealworms, crickets, roaches, silkworms.

The fat in the diet can be primarily given by the various insects. They are good sources of fat. Various oils also help to keep the fat content optimal in the diet of the dwarf hamster.

The carbohydrates and fibres in the diet is supplemented by grains, vegetables and fruits.

To meet his nutritional requirements, you might also have to give him certain supplements. The supplements will help you to make up for the essential nutrients that are not found in his daily meals.

Though these supplements are easily available, you should definitely consult a veterinarian before you give your dwarf hamster any kind of supplements.

You also have the option of giving commercial dwarf hamster food to your pet animal. But, it should be noted that no dwarf hamster food is complete in its nutritional requirements.

It is often believed that most commercial dwarf hamster foods are only equivalent to low quality cat food in their nutritional content. This is not good for the dwarf hamster's overall development.

They contain big pieces of fried fruits and nuts, which are difficult for the pet animal to chew. There have been many incidents of malnourished dwarf hamsters because of constant feeding of low quality cat food.

2. The everyday diet of the dwarf hamster

As discussed in the previous section, you can look at including good quality cat food or dog food as the main food of the dwarf hamster.

There has always been a debate about the right food for the pet dwarf hamster. The pet dwarf hamster's diet is so different from the wild dwarf hamster that it is all the more important to understand it well.

It is always recommended that the everyday diet of the dwarf hamster is closely worked out with a vet. This will help you to provide optimal nutrition to the pet animal.

A pet dwarf hamster who weights around 500 – 700 grams needs about 100 calories every night. This will vary based on the age and also health of the animal.

It is also important to provide the animal with adequate amounts of calcium and magnesium. You should try to mix fresh fruits and vegetables with the usual food, insects and mealworms.

If you find it cumbersome to cut fruits and veggies into small sizes, you can cut a big batch and freeze it. You can also buy baby food containing veggies and fruits and mix it with the cat food.

Vitamins and supplements

You should aim at providing all the necessary nutrients to the pet through his food. In such a case, you can avoid giving any extra supplements to the dwarf hamster.

At times, your dwarf hamster's diet might not be able to provide it with the right set of nutrients and vitamins. In such a case, it becomes necessary to introduce supplements in the diet of the pet animal.

It is always better to consult a veterinarian before you administer any vitamin or supplement to the dwarf hamster. You should also discuss the dosage with the veterinarian.

If the pet is not well and is recuperating from an injury or disease, the veterinarian might advise you to administer certain supplements to the pet. These supplements will help the pet to heal faster and get back on his feet sooner.

There are many vitamin supplements that are available in tasty treat forms for the dwarf hamster. While you can be sure that your pet is getting the right nutrients, the pet can enjoy the treat given to him.

You can also include supplements of fatty acids in the diet of the dwarf hamster. A few drops of this kind of supplement will enhance the taste and the nutritional value of the food item that is being served to the pet animal.

While it can be necessary to supplement certain vitamins and nutrients to the pet, you should also be aware of the hazards of over feeding a certain nutrient. If there is an overdose of a certain vitamin in the body of the dwarf hamster, it can lead to vitamin toxicity.

You might even see that your pet is enjoying all the supplements, but this in no way means that you can give him an overdose. You should always do what is right for the dwarf hamster's health.

It is advised to avoid various yogurt dips and salt licks that are available in various pet shops. You should also avoid supplements that are given to other small animals. The rule should be to look for supplements that can work even for a human being.

Insects

Dwarf hamsters feed themselves on insects in the wild. Many owners wonder whether it is necessary to feed the pet dwarf hamster with insects.

You can choose to serve insects to a pet dwarf hamster, but it is not necessary. If the pet is being served high quality nutritional food, he can do without the insects.

The main benefit of adding insects in the dwarf hamster's diet is that the insects will add a lot of fibre in the pet's diet. Eating insects also gives the pet the mental stimulation of hunting for prey in the wild.

If you decide to feed insects to the dwarf hamster, then you should look for insects that are smaller than a quarter size and are bred for pet food. These insects are safe and healthy for the pet animal.

You should avoid bugs that are being raised for bait. These bugs aren't very hygienic because of their poor sanitary conditions. Such a feed will only make the pet sick.

The insects those are safe for the dwarf hamster if they are bred for pets are wax worms, crickets, phoenix worms, hissing roaches, horn worms, mealworm beetle, mealworm pupae and mealworm larvae.

3. How much should you feed the dwarf hamster?
It is recommended that you keep a bowl of food available for the pet at all times. If your pet is not well and the vet has advised you to feed him less, then you can alter the quantities of food items that you serve him.

There are many owners who decrease the quantity of food they feed the pet animal with if he happens to gain some weight. You are advised not to do so. This can be detrimental for the health of the pet.

If your dwarf hamster has gained some weight, you should focus on increasing the amount of exercise that he gets. Don't deprive him of his food. This will have a negative effect on the health of the dwarf hamster.

Good exercise and food with a fat percentage less than 15 per cent are enough for the dwarf hamster to lose weight and remain healthy. You can also expect a relatively younger dwarf hamster to eat more than the adults.

A dwarf hamster eats one to four tablespoons of kibble at night. The amount he eats would be dependent on the size of the kibble. If the food has extra fillers, the dwarf hamster is expected to eat more and also defecate more.

It is said that the first sign of health issues in a dwarf hamster is a change in his appetite. You should always keep an eye on whether the pet is eating well or not.

A simple way to keep track of the dwarf hamster's diet is to count the number of kibble he eats. If you see any abrupt change in his food habits, you should consult the doctor. It is always better to catch a health problem in the earliest stages.

4. Switching foods

It is important to do the switching between various foods slowly and gradually. If you wish to add new foods to the diet of the dwarf hamster, even that needs to be slow.

If the shift is too sudden, the pet can develop health issues. A dwarf hamster can develop diarrhoea and the problem of green stools very easily.

It would take you time to understand the diet preferences of the dwarf hamster. These animals form their preferences quite early in their lives. If your dwarf hamster likes three kinds of food items instead of one, it gets easier for you also.

This means that the first few months is a great time for you to introduce different kinds of foods to the pet. This will help him to have his preferences and will also make things easier for you.

In case a certain food item is not available, you know that you have other choices. If you don't introduce new foods to the dwarf hamster, he will turn out to be a very fussy eater. And, you the parent will have a hard time keeping him happy.

If you wish to add more than one food to the diet, you should do it one at a time. It is important to observe if your pet is taking well to the new foods. The pet might have an allergy to certain items that you could be oblivious about.

The best way to introduce a new food item is to add a small quantity and gradually increase it. Also, observe carefully for at least a week for any signs of allergy from the pet animal.

If you wish to make a complete switch in the food that is being given to the dwarf hamster, then you should do it over a period of four to five weeks.

In week one, serve the dwarf hamster with his regular food and over seven or eight kibble of new food as a treat. In the second week, increase the quantity of the new food and make it one-fourth of the feed.

In the third week, serve half of the regular food and half of the new food. In the fourth week, reduce the quantity of the regular old food to one-fourth of

68

the feed. In the fifth week, you can expect the animal to be eating a full serving of the new food.

During the switch, observe the eating patterns of the dwarf hamster. Don't force him to eat anything and don't ignore any symptoms of allergy towards the new food.

There are some dwarf hamsters who will take to the transition easily, while others will completely discard the new food. You will have to introduce the new food in powdered form over the old food in such cases.

5. Treats

You should also offer treats to the pet animal every now and then. It is important that the treats are healthy. They should not disturb the nutritional balance of the pet animal.

If you keep serving him the wrong kinds of treats, it will only affect his health in the long run. It is also important that the pet associates the treat with reward. He should know that he is being served the treat reward for a reason.

You will have to keep a check on the amount of treats a pet will get. This is important because treats are not food replacements. They are only small rewards.

You should always look for treats that are healthy for the pet. The pet should enjoy eating them, but their nutrition should not be compromised.

When you serve the treat, you need to make sure that you don't add any extra salt or sugar. Also, make sure that you cut the food item into small pieces. It should preferably be in the size of a pea. It will be easier for the dwarf hamster to eat it.

It should be noted that just because your pet animal seems to enjoy a treat, you can't give the food item to him all day long. You will have to keep a check on the amount of treats a dwarf hamster will get. This is important because treats are not food replacements.

If you keep serving him the wrong kinds of treats, it will only affect his health in the long run. The pet can suffer from diarrhoea and other gastro intestinal problems because of consuming wrong food items. This is the last thing that you would want as a parent of the pet.

This section will help you understand various kinds of treats that you can serve your pet. The best kind of treat for a dwarf hamster is a food item that has meat as its main component. Dwarf hamsters will love it, and it is also healthy for them.

The following treats can be given to the dwarf hamster:

- **Insects**: Insects can be served as treats to the pet.

- **Yogurt without sugar and cottage cheese**: Though a dwarf hamster is lactose intolerant, these foods can be given in small quantities.

- **Various vegetables**: Various vegetables such as carrot, asparagus, bell pepper, celery, peas, sprouts and spinach can be given to the pet.

- **Various fruits**: Various fruits such as plum, pear, peach, kiwi, banana, apple, strawberry, raspberry, black berry and water melon can be given to the pet.

- **Meat**: Unseasoned meat items can be served to the dwarf hamster. You can serve items such as fish, lamb and chicken. You can boil it, roast it or bake it.

- **Baby food**: You can serve Gerber meat sticks and also sweet potatoes to the pet animal.

- **Eggs**: Unseasoned eggs serve as an excellent treat. You should cook the eggs properly before serving.

- **Wet cat food**: This food item is rich in proteins and fats. A good quality wet cat food that does not have preservatives can be given to the dwarf hamster.

6. Foods that should be avoided

There are certain food items that should be avoided for the dwarf hamster. This section will help you understand these food items.

Keep the food simple and healthy. If you are giving meat, then you should make sure that it should not have bones because the bones can get stuck in the throat of the animal.

Your pet wouldn't know that these foods are not good for him. You should take it upon yourself to keep such foods away from the pet.

If you are looking for a comprehensive list of food items that are unhealthy for the pet dwarf hamster, then the given list will help you. You should try to avoid these food items:

- **Corn**: Corn does not provide any nutrition to the pet dwarf hamster. It is important that you avoid this food type in any form whatsoever.

- **Sweeteners**: It is important to avoid corn syrup and sugar coated food.

- **Artificial preservatives**: They will add nothing to the diet of the pet. And, they are not good in the long run.

- **By products**: You should always try to give the real thing. There is no need to serve by products.

- **Caffeine**: You should keep tea and coffee away from your beloved pet. Sometimes, the children of the house can force the pet to consume such food items just for some fun. So, it is important that you keep a check on what the kids are doing when they are with the dwarf hamster.

- **Citrus fruits**: Citrus fruits such as lemons, pineapple, oranges and limes are not suitable for a pet dwarf hamster.

- **Chocolates**: Chocolates are unhealthy for dwarf hamsters. You should make sure that you keep these food items away from your dwarf hamster.

- Certain food items such as **onion and garlic**.

- **Raisins and grapes**: Though it is suggested that some fruits should be given to the pet dwarf hamster on a regular basis, grapes are not good for him. Grapes and raisins are toxic for the pet. If these food items are given for a longer duration, substantial damage is done to his health.

- **Most dried fruits**: Another food item that is dangerous for the pet animal is dried fruits. You might believe that they are healthy foods, so they should be fine for your pet also. But, this is not true. The pet dwarf hamster can choke on these dried fruits.

- **Avocado:** Another food item that is dangerous for the dwarf hamster is the avocado. The digestive system of the pet animal is not suited to digest this food item. The pet animal will experience diarrhoea and vomits after it consumes this food. It is extremely toxic for him.

- **Peanuts:** Another food item that is dangerous for the dwarf hamster is the peanuts. Other legumes should also not be given to the dwarf hamster. They can cause choking and vomiting pet.

- **Foods high in salt**: You should try not to feed foods that are very rich in salt content. You should keep all human junk food such as salted chips and nuts away from the pet dwarf hamster.

Chapter 6: Exercise for the dwarf hamster

Exercise is a very crucial activity for the well-being of the dwarf hamster. A dwarf hamster has too much energy which needs to be released in the right way.

As the parent of the pet, you should make sure that your pet dwarf hamster is given the right amount of a physical activity on a daily basis.

There are various ways to include optimum amounts of physical activity in a dwarf hamster's routine. This chapter will help you to understand these ways in greater detail.

1. Exercise wheel

An exercise wheel is a must have for all dwarf hamsters. A dwarf hamster can easily run for miles every night with the help of the exercise wheel. These are easily available at all local shops.

A dwarf hamster needs to release his energy. If he does not have an exercise wheel, you might find him running in circles in his space. He might also try to use other objects to release his energy.

The dwarf hamster might also just decide to take rest and sleep if there is no exercise wheel available for him. This will lead to an increase of weight in the pet, which in turn is the root cause of many health issues.

It is important that the exercise wheel is at least twelve inches in diameter. This will allow the dwarf hamster to exercise well without injuring himself while running.

You should try to get a bigger wheel, so that it is useful even when the dwarf hamster grows. A smaller wheel might induce back problems in a dwarf hamster.

The dwarf hamster might also lose interest in running and walking completely if the size of the wheel does not suit his size. The wheel should ideally have a diameter of twelve inches or even more.

The surface of the exercise wheel should be solid. Crossbars and spokes are not ideal for the running surface and can be dangerous for the pet animal.

You might get some cheaper exercise wheels with wire mesh. These can be used for rodents, but not for dwarf hamsters. The toe nails of the animal can be stuck and subsequently pulled by the wire mesh exercise wheels.

You should understand that in comparison to dwarf hamsters, rodents are more quick and agile. What suits a rodent might not suit a dwarf hamster. A dwarf hamster can hurt himself and can break a limb because of crossbars on the wheels.

It is also important that the exercise wheel is easy to clean. You will have to clean it regularly to keep it hygienic for the dwarf hamster. So it only makes sense if it is easier to clean.

There are many commercially available exercise wheels. But, it is always better to get it custom made for the dwarf hamster. These might cost a bit more, but they are worth every penny. The dwarf hamster will be safe when using it and you will find it easier to clean.

Cleaning the exercise wheel

It is important that the exercise wheel is cleaned properly and regularly. The dwarf hamster has a habit of defecating on the exercise wheel. The sad part is that you can't train him against that.

It is only natural for the pet animal to defecate while he is running on the exercise wheel. It is advised to clean the wheel every day. If that is not possible for you, then cleaning once in two to three days is mandatory.

It is not hygienic for the dwarf hamster if you let him run and exercise on an exercise wheel that is covered by his faeces. This is only an invitation to infections and diseases.

There are a few ways that you can make sure that the exercise wheel is neat and clean at all times. The type of the wheel will also affect the cleaning process of the wheel.

You can clean the exercise wheel with vinegar or a detergent. Apart from a good detergent, you should invest in some good cleaning products and sanitizers.

This will be necessary because the smell of the faeces will be difficult to get rid of. You will need these cleaning products to eliminate the smell of faeces from the wheel.

2. Taking the dwarf hamster outside

You can also take your pet dwarf hamster out in the open to play and exercise. This can be fun for both the pet dwarf hamster and you.

But, when you do so it is important to take care of a few things. You need to take the necessary precautions.

The ground temperature will always be less than the temperature of the air. You should make sure that you let the dwarf hamster play only on warmer grounds and not cold ones.

You should make sure that the grass or plants around are not sprayed with pesticides. This can be harmful for the pet. The plants should also be safe for the pet.

You don't want your pet to feast on harmful insects and bugs in the garden, so take him to a place where there are no bugs and insects.

You should also be sure that the place does not have bigger animals. The dwarf hamster can get scared and might not play at all. It is also possible that the bigger animal tries to injure the pet.

It is important to make sure that the pet dwarf hamster is not scared. It is easy to spot a scared pet. If you see your pet being pushed up in a corner, you should know that something is not right. If he is making noises similar to a hiss then you should know that he is definitely scared.

While your dwarf hamster is playing, it is important to keep an eye on him to make sure that he safe and sound. You might be busy with some work, and before you know your pet might be walking into some real danger.

A pet dwarf hamster can have a very curious personality. He will not think twice before charging into unknown territory. You should know that the pet has a tendency to injure himself.

If you don't pay attention, the damage could be very serious and irrevocable. Don't let him go to areas where you can't keep a watchful eye on him.

3. Playpen

When an animal is very young, it is always advised to keep him under observation. He should be supervised by you at all times. In fact, it is better to keep an eye on the pet irrespective of how young or old he is.

Even if you are not around and are busy, then a family member should be around the dwarf hamster. After trying all possible means, if you still feel that there will be times when the dwarf hamster would be on its own for a while, then a playpen is a good option for you.

The use of the playpen can be very handy for you during the playtime of your dwarf hamster. The playpen will keep the animal safe and away from any danger.

A playpen is a small enclosure where the animal can be kept safely. It is portable so you can keep it wherever you want to. A playpen is also used for human infants. The infants can play in this enclosure, while the parents can be happy knowing that that infant is safe.

When you are choosing the best playpen for your pet, make sure that you choose a mesh playpen. This will be an injury free and safe option for the animal.

If the dwarf hamster is too scared to come out of his bed, you can let the pet be in his blanket. Keep the blanket with the pet in the playpen. This will keep him warm and safe.

It should be noted that if you have the option of the playpen, it definitely does not mean that you can keep the animal in the playpen all day long. You should try to keep the pet as close to you as possible. The playpen should be used only in case of emergency.

4. Toys

Though different animals have different personalities, dwarf hamsters are not much interested in toys. They don't get too excited by the prospect of playing with a toy.

Playing with toys can't be the main activity if you are looking for ways to exercise your pet. But, it can be an option that you can use sometimes. It is better to keep them as an option.

There are some dwarf hamsters that could be enthusiastic about toys. It will depend on your pet. But, mostly they will enjoy running. As the pet owner, you should make sure that the primary focus is always on running.

The pet dwarf hamster will not play the game of fetch with you. He will not do special acrobatics with you. But, he can have fun with some simple toys, which you can buy for him.

You should also make sure that the pet does not play with very small toys and toxic items. The pet might choke himself in an attempt to eat the stuff.

If you are looking at buying some toys for the dwarf hamster, then you can choose from toys such as stuffed toys for pets, tubes and pipes, balls and dig boxes. All these items will be a source of great amusement and fun for the dwarf hamster.

The right kind of toys should be bought for the pet animal. You will get many ideas when you visit a shop that keeps toys for the pet. But, it is important that the toys are made of good quality material.

They should not be harmful for the pet. Your pet animal will take them in his mouth, so they should be of a good quality. It is better if the toys are washable.

This will enable you to wash the pet animal's toys every now and then when they are dirty. The harmful bacteria will also be removed from the toys when they are washed.

Also, make sure that the toys cannot be shredded by the pet animal. If the pet is able to shred the toy, he will swallow the shreds. This is very harmful and will only invite more trouble for the pet.

To avoid all these issues, buy the right kind of toys. The toys of the pet should be washed once every two weeks, if the toys are washable.

If you take the dwarf hamster to an open space to play, make sure that you are in the vicinity. You don't want to lose the pet because of your negligence. It is important that you know what he is up to at all times.

It can be very difficult if a dwarf hamster hides and refuses to budge. This situation can be a nightmare for any owner. What if the dwarf hamster got lost and couldn't find the way?

To prepare yourself and your dwarf hamster better for such situations, you can try a simple and easy trick. Buy a few toys that make sound for your dwarf hamster.

This will allow you to know where the pet is playing with his toys. There are some easy and fun tips that will make the entire process very entertaining and fun for both of you.

Chapter 7: Training the dwarf hamster

The training phase can be a great opportunity for you to learn more about your little pet. No matter how much you read about a dwarf hamster, your pet will have some individual properties that will separate him from the rest of the lot.

The more you learn about your pet, the stronger bond you form with him. You should remember to not take the training phase as a cumbersome thing. In fact, take it as an opportunity to form an everlasting bond with your pet. Your pet will also understand you better during this time.

Though the dwarf hamster has been domesticated for years, you have to train him to make him more suitable to your home.

When you are training a pet, it is important that you monitor the progress of your pet from time to time. This is important so that you know whether the pet is making any improvements or not.

When you know what you can expect from a new pet, it gets easier. Try to understand that he is still uncomfortable in the new surroundings and will require some time to get used to all that is new around him.

Give him that space, time and also your understanding. The training will also require you to be patient. You will have to do a few trial and errors before you can be sure that your dwarf hamster is well trained.

1. What to do if the pet is not responding to training?
You should remember that the dwarf hamster needs to feel comfortable and secure in your presence. You should spend quality time with him. Don't put him in the cage unnecessarily.

If he is left in the cage unattended all the time, he will become depressed. You have to be compassionate and kind towards the pet. Treat him when he exhibits good behaviour. This will encourage him further.

A simple reason that could be behind your pet not responding well to your training session is that the dwarf hamster is sick. You have to know your pet well to be able to detect sudden changes in his behaviour.

If you see the pet being aggressive or defensive when you try to play with him, he could be sick. You should thoroughly examine your pet for any injuries.

If you spot an injury, you should take him to the veterinarian. If he looks sick and tired, even then it is a good idea to take him to the veterinarian. You should never postpone such things because this will drastically affect the pet's health.

It is also important to be realistic when you are trying to train your pet. You can't expect to train him for things that don't come easily to him.

For example, you can train the pet not to bite and to litter in the box, but you can't train him to be a dog. You can't expect him to go fetch the ball for you. This will only lead to disappointment for you.

The dwarf hamster can roll into a ball and probably push certain things. He will run for you. But, if you are expecting him to learn complicated tricks then you will have a very hard time.

The dwarf hamster's brain is not advanced to learn such things. Even if you succeed to a certain degree, you can expect the pet to unlearn everything that you taught at any time.

2. Training against biting

It is known that a dwarf hamster does not bite much, and not all dwarf hamsters bite. But, a scared or excited dwarf hamster can bite you. This can be hurtful for you.

This can be uncomfortable and worrisome for you as the owner. But, you should know that this is absolutely normal for a dwarf hamster and that you can slowly train the animal not to exhibit such behaviour.

Such behaviour is quite common in younger dwarf hamsters. The younger dwarf hamster is trying to adjust. So, don't be surprised when the young animal bites you really hard.

The animal could be scared. When you bring the pet to your home for the first time, everything around him will be new. It is quite natural for the pet to get scared.

It should be noted that if the dwarf hamster has had a history of abuse, then you can expect him to bite more in fear than in a playful mood. If the dwarf hamster bites you really hard you can have a real bad wound. This makes it all the more important to train the pet.

The first and foremost thing that you should remember is that you should not harm the pet when he bites. This could scare him and will make things worse for you. If you mishandle the pet and try to beat him up, he might also try to bite you and harm.

If you beat him or give him punishment, the dwarf hamster will associate it with something bad and scary in his head. You might not realize, but slowly the pet will start avoiding you.

A simple trick to help the dwarf hamster understand that he can't bite is to hold him and drag him away from you. You need to establish the fact that you are the dominant one in the house.

When you are pulling the dwarf hamster away, you need to be very careful. You want to train the pet and not harm him. Use your thumb and the index finger to hold the skin at the back of the dwarf hamster's neck. In this way, you will be able to hold easily.

Look for the reactions of the dwarf hamster. He should not be in pain. The idea is to teach him to give up biting. When you hold him at the back of his neck, gently push him away from you.

You might have to repeat this action several times before the animal understands what is expected of him. Another point that you need to know while training your pet is that you need to monitor your actions too.

You need to figure out whether biting is a habit with the pet or has he suddenly started. If the pet has recently started, then it could be something related to you.

It could be the smell of the new lotion that you started using or the smell of the new perfume that you started using. Dwarf hamsters can get attracted to fragrances and this can lead to biting. You will have to figure out these things to train your pet well.

3. Litter training

Litter training is also an important part of pet training and grooming. If the pet is allowed to defecate anywhere, it can be a nightmare for you. You will have to spend the day chasing the pet to clean his faeces.

Don't get upset when you see your pet dwarf hamster littering all around. You can train him to not do so. This will take time and will also require you to be patient. There are many owners that insist on litter training.

As the owner, you are also the care taker and the parent for the pet. You will have to teach him stuff that he needs to know when living in a family. If you wish to litter train your pet, you will have to buy the required products for the same.

As you might have understood by now, the dwarf hamster is very fond of digging up places. He might not leave the litter box. A dwarf hamster digging up a litter box is not something very hygienic. You will have to adopt some tips to stop your pet animal from digging in the litter box.

If the box is very clean, it could be like an invitation to the pet animal to come and dig. You can try keeping some paper litter in the box, so that the dwarf hamster stays away from it.

When the pet animal approaches such a place, he will smell something different. The smell will tell him that this place is not to dig. The pet animal might take some time, but will finally understand it.

Another way to reduce the behaviour of digging anywhere is to get a sand box for the pet animal. You will find it easily at the pet shop that houses dwarf hamster related products. This box will give the animal a designated place to dig. This will reduce the impulse of the pet to dig every place.

Litter training is essential for all captive animals. No pet parent wants to be surprised by litter or faeces from the pet every morning. This will make you hate your pet more than you love him.

You should buy a few litter boxes. You can also prepare your own with a simple cardboard or plastic boxes. The idea is to give the dwarf hamster a designated place to relieve himself.

Keep these boxes in various areas of the house where the dwarf hamster is most likely to litter. You should cover the various corners where you have found the litter earlier. Also, install one box in the cage. Eventually, you want the pet to litter in the cage itself.

There is a chance that the pet dwarf hamster will relieve himself first thing in the morning. So, there is a chance that the pet has already littered in the box in the cage. When you open the cage to take him out, check the box and wait till has used the box.

When the dwarf hamster understands that you will let him out of the cage once he uses the litter box, he might pretend to use it. You need to check the box and make sure that he has actually used it.

You should signal the dwarf hamster by pointing towards the litter box. The pet should slowly realize that he needs to use the box if he wants to get out of the cage. You should wait near the cage till he is all done.

If you notice that the pet is not using the litter box installed in his cage, then you need to understand why. There is a chance that the litter box is uncomfortable for him. In such a case, you should look to buy a box which is bigger. This will be better for the dwarf hamster.

The litter box should definitely be bought considering the weight and size of the dwarf hamster. The pet animal should be comfortable using the litter box. You can also buy a cat litter box. You will notice that the front ledge is not low enough is such boxes.

You could cut in in half to make it suitable for your dwarf hamster. The idea is to make it really comfortable for your pet dwarf hamster. A suitable litter box will have a back that is high. This gives the right support to the pet.

The dwarf hamster will take its own good time to adjust with the environment. It is always difficult for a new pet to adjust. If you get him a new cage or if you make any changes in his surroundings, he will find it difficult to adjust.

But, this problem is only time related and will get solved. Every time the pet animal litters outside the box, place his litter in the box that he should be using.

You need to show the pet that he should be using the litter box. This could be difficult for you in the beginning, but the pet animal will learn soon enough. You should place food and toys in areas and corners that you want to save.

When the pet sees a toy or a food item in a corner, he will try to look for another corner to pass his stools. You can also place a mat underneath the litter box to save your carpet or home mats. Make sure that the mat that you use is water proof.

Observe your dwarf hamster's mannerisms when he is using the litter box. If he has a tendency to bite the mat underneath or stuff kept around, you should discourage this behaviour.

If you notice that the pet is not using the litter box at all, then you need to understand why. There is a chance that the litter box is uncomfortable for him.

The litter box of the pet dwarf hamster should definitely be kept clean to maintain the overall hygiene and to prevent diseases. You should wash the box a few times every week.

The pet will also use its sense of smell to use the areas that he has used before. You should leave some paper litter in the box to encourage the pet to use the box again. This is a simple trick that you can use when you are trying to litter train your pet.

If you have more than one pet in your home then you should make sure that each pet has his own box, so that he is not left to use the carpets and the floors. Even after you have trained your dwarf hamster to use the litter box, you have to be vigilant.

He might still not use it every time. This can be frustrating for you, but it is important that you maintain your cool and don't get angry at the pet. You should keep training him without getting angry.

If you are observant, you will have to face fewer issues. There could be instances when your pet would suddenly give up the use of the litter box. Instead of getting angry with him, it is important that you probe into the reason for his sudden change in behaviour.

When the pet dwarf hamster is sick, he might give up the use of the litter box. The main reason behind this is that the pet might not have the strength in his legs to get on to the box.

He could be suffering from an infection or disease, which could make him weak and lethargic. It is important to look for signals.

You should be cautious when you observe such changes in your pet. Don't ignore his condition, or don't force him to use the litter box. You should not get angry at the pet because he is littering on the floor. It is not his fault if he is not well.

The best thing to do in such a situation is to take the pet to the vet. This will avoid the condition from getting worse. He will look for the symptoms of various diseases and will help you to understand what is wrong with the pet.

Chapter 8: Maintaining the health of the dwarf hamster

Maintaining the health of the dwarf hamster would always be your primary concern as the owner. The food that you give him, his environment, his hygiene levels, everything will ultimately affect his health.

This chapter will help you to understand simple ways to keep the dwarf hamster healthy. You will also learn about the common health problems that can affect your dwarf hamster.

You should always make sure that your pet dwarf hamster is always kept in a clean environment. A neat and clean environment will help you to keep away many common ailments and diseases.

You should understand the various health related issues that your pet can suffer from. This knowledge will help you to get the right treatment at the right time.

It is also important that you understand how you can take care of a sick pet. This knowledge will help you to keep your pet calm and help the sick animal in the best way possible. Proper care will help him to get better faster.

1. Maintaining records

It is advised to maintain regular health records for your pet. This will help you to understand his health in a better way. You would be able to detect even the smallest of issues with the help of these records.

For example, if you have a record of his weight, you can notice any changes in the pet's weight. A drastic change in weight is often understood as an early symptom of diseases.

This can help you to take further actions such as taking the pet to the veterinarian for a check-up. The pet can be saved from future health issues by keeping a simple record.

If you can't keep a daily record, aim at a weekly record. Record all the important parameters at the beginning of each week and compare with the previous week.

The parameters that you should be aiming to record are the weight of the pet, the physical activity or wheeling of the pet and the food intake of the pet.

You can calculate the quantity of food that the pet consumes by counting the number of kibble or by weighing the food that you serve and then the food that is left.

You can record the wheeling activity by observing and estimating the time. To make it accurate, you can attach a bike computer to his exercise wheel. This bike computer will record the parameters for you.

You should also look out for any gunk formation or lump formation on the body of the pet. You should also make sure that there are no trappings of hair around the limbs of the pet.

A lethargic pet that shows no interest in wheeling is not a good sign. You will only know these things if you observe. If you notice any change in the pet's normal activity levels or weight, you should be alerted.

This definitely means that something is wrong with the pet. An early action can save you from many health problems in the pet. This is good both for you and the pet.

2. First aid

The main aim of first aid is to give the pet some relief from his pain. Giving first aid would not be very difficult if you follow the right steps in the right order.

While you are giving the animal some first aid, there are a few things that you should do. This will help you to calm the dwarf hamster and also give him the necessary aid.

You should make sure that you don't aggravate the pain and misery of the poor animal in any way. You should follow the given procedures in the given order to help the dwarf hamster.

You should make sure that the airway of the animal is not blocked. Make sure that the dwarf hamster is able to breathe properly.

After you have made sure that the animal is breathing properly, it is important to check if he bleeding. If the animal is bleeding, you should take the necessary steps to stop his bleeding.

You should also be able to examine how profusely he is bleeding. After you have succeeded in reducing the bleeding of the dwarf hamster, you have to take the necessary steps to maintain the right temperature of the pet animal.

If the body temperature is not maintained, it will worsen the condition of the pet. You should understand that dwarf hamster is easily prone to stress. Injury and pain are two factors that can stress him a lot.

So, it is important that you take the necessary steps to reduce his stress levels. This might seem like an impossible and daunting task, but if you take the right steps, you will be able to calm your animal successfully.

When you keep a first aid kit, it is important that you have knowledge about each item. You should know how to use things. You should also replace stuff when they reach their expiration date.

For an upset stomach, you can keep canned pumpkin or acidophilus. If the dwarf hamster develops dry ears, you can use lanolin. Chlorhexidine solution can be used as a disinfectant.

The various items that the first aid box of the dwarf hamster should have are bottled water, hand warmers, paper towels, flash light, toilet paper, scissors, tweezers, nail clippers, cotton swabs, hydrogen peroxide, saline water, vitamin A cream, vitamin D cream, Neosporin, Pedialyte and ensure.

3. When should you see the veterinarian?
If you find your pet behaving different from normal, then the first step you should take is to provide him warmth. It is important that the pet is not cold and that a proper temperature is maintained.

Even after that if you see him deteriorating, it is time to see the veterinarian. If the condition is not very severe, you can book an appointment in the next three to four days.

But if there is an emergency, you should not waste time and should take the dwarf hamster to the veterinarian as soon as possible. You can also take him to the emergency clinic in your locality.

It is important that you are able to identify the signs of emergency in your pet so that you can get treatment without delay. If you happen to notice the following in your pet dwarf hamster, you should know that it is an emergency and the veterinarian needs to be consulted:

- **Lethargy**: If the pet is not moving at all, try to increase the heat for him. If the pet remains unresponsive even after that, this can be serious. Don't do something drastic such as sprinkling water over him. Just take him to the vet.

- **Diarrhoea**: If the problem of diarrhoea or green stools persists for more than two days, you will have to get a fecal exam done for any complications.

- **Blood**: Blood from a bloody toe or from a small cut is not a thing to worry about. But, blood from urine or the nose or mouth is a cause of serious concern. The female has no period, so don't expect any blood from the female pet as her period.

- **Runny nose**: Sneezing and runny nose are symptoms of respiratory disease. It can get critical if not treated on time.

- **Vomit**: Vomit caused by poisoning, choking or sickness should not be ignored at any cost.

- If you see the pet gasping for breath, or if you notice twitching or abnormal movements of limbs, you should consult the veterinarian as soon as possible.

4. Common diseases in dwarf hamsters

An unhealthy pet can be a nightmare for any owner. The last thing that you would want is to see your pet lying down in pain. Many disease causing parasites dwell in unhygienic places and food.

If you take care of the hygiene and food of the dwarf hamster, there are many diseases that can be averted. You should always consult a vet when you find any unusual traits and symptoms in the pet.

You should make sure that the dwarf hamster has all his vaccines on time. Apart from this, you should take him for regular check-ups to the veterinarian. This is important so that even the smallest health issue can be tracked at an early stage.

At times, even after all the precautions that you take, the pet can get sick. It is always better to be well equipped so that you can help your pet.

A pet dwarf hamster is prone to certain diseases such as urinary tract infections and obesity. If proper care is not taken, you will find your pet getting sick very often.

Another point that needs to be noted here is that a dwarf hamster has a tendency to fall sick, but can easily hide the sickness from you. You will have to be extra vigilant to understand that something is wrong with the pet.

This section will help you to understand the various diseases that a dwarf hamster can suffer from. The various symptoms and causes are also discussed in detail. This will help you to recognize a symptom, which should have otherwise gone unnoticed.

Though this section helps you to understand the various common health problems of the dwarf hamster, it should be understood that a veterinarian should be consulted in case of any health related issue. A veterinarian will physically examine the pet and suggest what is best for your pet animal.

The various diseases that your pet dwarf hamster can suffer from are as follows:

Obesity

A dwarf hamster is highly prone to obesity. There are two main causes of obesity in dwarf hamsters. Either the animal is not getting proper exercise or he is genetically prone to obesity.

An obese dwarf hamster will have bulges in his armpit areas and shoulder areas. He will also find it difficult to roll into a ball like other dwarf hamsters.

It should be noted that there is no single ideal weight for a dwarf hamster. Your dwarf hamster could be 400gms and overweight and he can be 600gms and healthy.

The main criteria for a healthy weight are that the pet should look well proportioned. He should be able to roll into a ball. Also, he should be eating healthy and exercising well.

Treatment:

In case of genetically obese dwarf hamsters, it will be difficult to control obesity in spite of your best efforts. You can take care of the pet's diet and encourage him to exercise.

You should plan regular visits to the veterinarian to make sure there are no complications arising from the obese condition of the pet dwarf hamster.

If the dwarf hamster has gained weight because of a lethargic lifestyle, then you need to make sure that the animal starts exercising regularly on the exercise wheel.

You should not make the mistake of decreasing the quantity of the food that the dwarf hamster consumes. You should concentrate on the fat content of the food and make sure it is just right for him.

Gastrointestinal blockage

The pet might accidentally swallow something dangerous for him, such as a foam or rubber piece. This will cause the blockage of the digestive tract in the animal.

Gastrointestinal blockage is a very common problem in dwarf hamsters. It is even said that it is one of the main causes behind premature death in dwarf hamsters. This condition occurs when the animal has a case of swollen intestinal tissue.

You can look out for the various symptoms in the dwarf hamster to know that he is suffering from this particular disease. The pet will lose his appetite. You will find him avoiding even his favourite foods.

He will not drink water, which could further lead to dehydration. You will also notice a sudden and drastic weight loss in the pet. Another symptom of this disorder is vomiting. The pet will throw up from time to time.

The pet would be seen struggling during his bowel movements. You should watch out for this symptom. You will notice the pet to be very lazy and lethargic. The pet could suffer from acute diarrhoea.

Treatment:

If you find any of the above symptoms in your pet dwarf hamster, it is important that you waste no time and take the pet to the veterinarian. The vet will conduct an X-ray and ultrasound to confirm the blockage. Don't make the mistake of treating the pet at home.

Usually the symptoms start with vomiting. Severe dehydration follows the bouts of vomiting. If there is a blockage, the animal would need surgery. It is important that you are mentally prepared for this.

The best way to avoid such incidents is to always keep an eye on the pet. The dwarf hamster is a curious animal. He would always be running into some kind of trouble if you don't have an eye on him.

You should make sure that all dangerous items, such as rubber items and foam items are not in the reach of the pet. Such a blockage ruptures the intestinal tissue, making digestion of food very difficult for the pet.

Keeping dangerous things out of the sight of the pet is probably the best way to avert all the tension that arises following a gastrointestinal blockage.

Dry skin

Dwarf hamsters tend to suffer from the issue of dry skin many a times. Dry skin is categorised by flaky skin. Some people mistake it for an infestation of mites.

If you attempt to look through the hairs of the animal, you may see dry and loose flakes of skin. This is the main test of dry skin.

There are a few causes that can lead to dry skin, such as improper diet, excessive bathing, dry surroundings and particulate beddings.

Treatment:

The best bet to treat dry skin in your dwarf hamster is to apply flax seed oil to the affected areas. The oil will help the skin to heal and will also let the skin breathe. It will also wash off easily.

You can also use olive oil capsules or vitamin E oil. These oils are easily available in all health stores. You can apply the oils directly on the affected areas, or you can also put two to three drops in his food.

Continuous use of good quality oil will show you excellent results in a few weeks. Pour two to three drops of the oil at least once a week in the food bowl of the pet.

You can also give the pet a bath. While you bathe him, make use of a soft pet brush to gently scrape off the loose and dry skin.

It is also highly advised that you buy a mist humidifier. This will keep the air warm and humidity up. When a dwarf hamster experiences low humidity levels, he can easily get dry skin.

If the problem does not end after all these measures, it is advised to get a skin scrape done by the veterinarian. This will help you to determine if there is more to the problem than what you understand.

Tumours and cysts

Your pet is also at risk of various cysts and tumours. If you notice any bumps on the body of the dwarf hamster, don't take it lightly. This can be dangerous.

It occurs because of the uncontrolled growth of the cells in the dwarf hamster's body. Though this is very common in these animals, it can be difficult to detect, especially in the earlier stages.

It is known that older dwarf hamsters are more at risk of such tumours and cysts. But, various tumours can also attack younger dwarf hamsters.

You should never take any symptom lightly and should visit the veterinarian when you observe changes in a dwarf hamster. The veterinarian will conduct tests on the blood sample of the pet to confirm this health condition.

You can look out for the various common symptoms in the dwarf hamster to know that he is suffering from this particular disease. You will notice sudden and drastic weight loss in the pet.

You will notice the pet to be very lazy and lethargic. It will appear that he has no energy to do anything. The pet will have visible bumps and changes in the skin texture.

The pet will suffer from diarrhoea. The lymph nodes of the pet will also be swollen.

Another symptom that could accompany this disease is a cough. The pet will experience some difficulty in his breathing and will acquire a bad cough.

Treatment:

It is important that you take the pet to the veterinarian. He will be able to administer certain medicines and injections. The veterinarian might also suggest surgery.

It is very difficult to save the pet after he has been diagnosed with this deadly tumour. Mostly, it gets detected in later stages, so the treatment becomes all the more difficult.

Because the symptoms of this disease are very general, it is suggested that you ask your veterinarian to conduct yearly tests for your pet.

This would help in detecting any issue in the very beginning, which makes it possible to treat it successfully.

Infestation with mites

Dwarf hamsters are also prone to mites. Mites can lead to skin irritation in the beginning and then severe skin allergy if not treated. The inflammation of the skin because of the infection caused by mites makes the dwarf hamster irritable and restless.

It is not a very deadly disease and can be controlled easily with the help of a few precautions and measures. Once the pet acquires this disease, it keeps spreading if the condition is not treated.

It is a skin disease, so a change in the texture of the skin on the pet could be an indication of an infection. In most cases, the skin starts getting red.

The pet will scratch again and again at one spot. You will find the pet to be very irritated and agitated. The skin could also develop rashes or scales.

Treatment:

Like other pet animals, dwarf hamsters can also be attacked by mites easily. These mites can lead to skin diseases if not treated on time.

This skin disease can be treated by the use of mild medicated soaps. These soaps will soothe the skin and will also treat the infection.

There are some creams that can also help to treat the skin and make the condition better. In severe cases, the certain ointments might have to be applied to the skin. You should also take care of the diet of the pet.

A good diet will help the skin to heal itself faster. In the case that, the skin gets worse with passing time then you will have to consult the veterinarian. He might suggest some oral medicines to heal the skin faster.

He might also suggest some special ointments that will give some relief to the pet. The use of 'Revolution' is recommended for the dwarf hamsters. It helps the skin to get rid of mites faster.

Ivermectin is one medicine that you should try to avoid because it has more side effects than benefits.

Bloody feet

There is a chance that a dwarf hamster is so lazy and obese that it is difficult to make him exercise. On the other hand, there is also a probability that the pet might exercise so much that he might get bloody feet.

The dwarf hamster can run so much on his exercise wheel that his feet can get all raw. If the exercise wheel has a groove that is raised, there is a higher chance of your dwarf hamster injuring himself.

If a nail of the dwarf hamster gets stuck somewhere, even then he can get bloody feet.

If you are not particular about cleaning the feet of the dwarf hamster then certain bacteria can break in through the skin and cause bloody feet. This will be very uncomfortable for the pet dwarf hamster.

Treatment:

It is known that bloody feet are easy to treat. If the right treatment is given at the right time, the pet dwarf hamster does not have to suffer much.

You need to be cautious enough to know that the pet is suffering from this condition. Even if the bruise does not appear very severe, it is important to treat it before it becomes very bad.

Give the pet a warm water foot bath to treat their feet. You can put a few drops of Vitamin E in the warm water for enhanced results. If you don't want to do this, then you can make the dwarf hamster walk on a wet towel.

You can remove the exercise wheel from the cage of the dwarf hamster. It is better if he does not strain his feet for a couple of nights.

You should also make sure that the cage is neat and clean. This is important so that no viruses or bacteria can irritate the dwarf hamster on his injured feet.

Urinary tract infection or UTI

An infection in the urinary tract of the animal is termed UTI. UTI in dwarf hamsters is quite similar to UTI in human beings. Various parasites can lead to UTI.

You should look out for symptoms such as blood in urine and also difficulty to pass urine. The pet will experience pain and will seem very uncomfortable.

Treatment:

If your pet is suffering from UTI, it is advised that you see the veterinarian as soon as possible. He will diagnose the dwarf hamster and advise medication accordingly.

If you have a female dwarf hamster, you will have to make sure that the infection that the pet has is urinary and is not uterine. Urine will have to be taken out from her bladder by fine needle aspiration to make the diagnosis clear.

It is always advised to hydrate the dwarf hamster well. This is a simple and effective way to prevent UTI.

6. Syringe feeding the dwarf hamster

When the pet dwarf hamster is sick, the vet might suggest that you syringe feed him. The pet might give up eating on his own, or he might not be in a condition to do so.

This makes it important that you are familiar with the concept of syringe feeding. You can use a syringe that is about 1-5ml. You also need a few paper towels when you are syringe feeding your pet.

Firstly, heat the food. It should not be too hot but warm enough for the dwarf hamster. You should carefully fill the syringe with the warm food.

Take paper towels and spread them nicely on your lap. You can also use an absorbent blanket instead of the paper towels.

After you are ready, gently hold the dwarf hamster and keep him in your lap. Make sure that the pet is not on his back because this will choke him when you are feeding him.

It is best to keep him in an upright position. If the pet is weak, give him support with your hand. Now, gently use the syringe to put some food in his mouth.

Feed him from the side of his mouth so that there are no chances of choking. Also, keep the quantity low and give him some time to swallow. Rub his chin to help him swallow.

Scruffing

While you are syringe feeding him or checking him for potential injuries, you can gently scruff the dwarf hamster. This will give you a better grip on the animal while you finish your task.

Hold the pet near the neck area with a very gentle hand. Use the other hand to give him support, or you can use your knee to give him support.

You won't be able to hold him in this position for too long because he will try to escape your grip. It is advised to check for injuries or syringe feed him a small amount quickly and let him go.

7. Taking care of a senior dwarf hamster

A dwarf hamster of age four or five is said to be an elderly or senior dwarf hamster. It is important to care for the pet as he grows old. He will show certain changes in his body and behaviour that you should be okay with.

It is not right to expect a senior dwarf hamster to have the same energy levels as a younger one. The senior pet will exercise less, eat less and litter less. They will start becoming oblivious of their routine light schedule.

The pet will also show a decline in his listening capacity and eyesight. The teeth will also show signs of decay. They will not be able to eat food items that require excessive chewing.

The pet will become lethargic. He will not have much energy and would prefer sleeping most of the time. He might sometimes litter in his bed so that he does not have to walk outside.

The dwarf hamster will also be stressed easily. Please don't force an elderly dwarf hamster to act young. You have to let him be if you wish to see him happy.

There are a few things that you need to take care of. Make sure that the pet has extra blankets at his disposal to keep his joints warm. You can also keep a heating pad under his bedding.

If you are using a heating pad, it is important to monitor it regularly. The heating pad can get too warm for the pet very quickly. This can be dangerous for the dwarf hamster.

You should also make sure that you mix kibble with water before serving that to him. You can also feed him canned food that is easier to eat. If the pet is losing excessive weight, feed him with fat rich food items.

If the pet is experiencing any kinds of pain, you should consult the veterinarian. He might prescribe some pain relief medication.

Though the pet will not show much inclination towards exercising, you should encourage him to do some everyday. You should also lower the exercise wheel so that he can get on the wheel easily.

It is important that you maintain daily health records of the pet. The pet should be healthy even when he is four years old. Schedule frequent visit to the veterinarian and make sure that the dwarf hamster remains fit.

8. Dwarf hamster insurance

Covering the medical needs of a pet is an integral part of pet care. A healthy pet is like an asset, but when the same pet falls ill, it can be a nightmare.

If you buy insurance to cover these conditions, you will save yourself from a lot of trouble. Depending on the insurance you buy, you can also cover the cost to pay for regular clinic visits. There are some companies that will give you discounts on clinic visits.

Getting insurance for the pet can help you to be tension free about the medical expenses that you might encounter while bringing him up. It is important that you plan this well in advance. This insurance will help you to take care of the vet bills, surgery and injury costs.

Like most other pet animals, dwarf hamsters have a tendency of getting sick very easily. It is known that by the time the disease is confirmed, the pet might need to be operated. They can also get injured. These procedures can cost you over thousands of pounds and dollars.

There are some companies that can help you with dwarf hamster insurance, such as Exotic direct. There are many kinds of wellness packages for the dwarf hamsters.

Make sure that you discuss the policy with the vet. The company that you choose to buy the insurance with will also take into account the health of your dwarf hamster. Each insurance policy will have a set of conditions that will have to be met.

You can choose according to your requirement. You can also get a package deal if you are looking to insure more than one dwarf hamster. When you buy insurance, you have to pay a deductible amount and regular premiums.

It is very important to understand the policy that you are buying. You should know which diseases are covered in the policy. There are some policies that provide security against only a few dwarf hamster diseases.

You will also be required to pay premiums that need to be paid regularly to keep the insurance policy active. The premium that you will pay will depend on the kind of insurance policy you opt for.

Buying a good policy can help you to cover $2716.50/£2000 in the given policy period. Both illness and injury will be covered in such policies. You can expect to pay a deductible amount of about $80/£58.90 per year to keep the policy alive.

9. Choosing a veterinarian

Don't wait for the pet to fall sick. It is always a good idea to choose a veterinarian for the animal in advance.

If your pet falls sick or encounters an injury, you should know where to take him. The last thing you want to do is to search for a vet when the pet's condition is deteriorating.

The best way to find a good veterinarian is to go by the breeder's suggestion. You should always choose the best breeder to buy your dwarf hamster from.

A good breeder will always consult a good vet, and will suggest the same to you. Take a few recommendations from your breeder who will help you when you are selecting a vet.

It is important that the veterinarian has good experience of working with dwarf hamsters. Many of them might have the knowledge, but might lack in practical experience. It is your duty to make sure that the vet holds a good name amongst other owners of dwarf hamsters.

While you are choosing your veterinarian, you should also consider the distance of his clinic and your home. You would want to consult a vet who is good and also closest to your home.

Chapter 9: Maintaining overall hygiene of the dwarf hamster

It is important to maintain overall hygiene of the pet. This is to avoid any future health related problems. A dwarf hamster falls into the category of self-grooming pets.

You don't have to spend too much time in grooming of the pet. An occasional bath and regular trimming of nails should be sufficient to groom the pet and maintain his hygiene.

1. Trimming nails

As the owner, you will have to make sure that the nails of the pet dwarf hamster are trimmed regularly. This is very important because longer nails can be troublesome both for the animal and the pet owner.

The long nails can get stuck in various places, causing discomfort to the pet dwarf hamster. They can also cause hindrance when the animal is on the exercise wheel.

In severe cases, the nails can even dig into the pads of the pet's feet. To avoid such painful incidents, it is important that your pet is comfortable with you touching his feet.

If your dwarf hamster is a cooperative one, then things can get easier. But, generally a dwarf hamster will not be as cooperative as you would want him to be.

To make things easier, you should make him comfortable with his feet being touched. When you are with the pet, make sure that you gently stroke his feet now and then.

Another option is to take the pet to the vet. The vet would sedate the animal. The sedation will allow the vet to trim the pet's nails easily.

A dwarf hamster needs nail trimming once in two to three weeks. It might not be possible for you to take the dwarf hamster to the veterinarian each time, so it better to practice it on your own.

If you have another person in your home who can help you, things can get easier. The person can hold the animal while you cut the nails. You don't have to cut all the nails in one sitting. You can do it as it suits you.

It is very important to understand how much you can trim a nail so that you don't hurt the animal. The nails of the dwarf hamster are similar to the nails of dogs and cats.

They have a pink coloured blood vessel 'quick', which is extremely sensitive. It is important to not touch this blood vessel otherwise it can be very painful for the dwarf hamster.

You can use cuticle clippers that are easily available. It is better to use nail clippers used for human babies. You should avoid the big animal nail clippers that are available in most pet stores.

If you cut the quick accidentally and blood starts to come out, you should comfort the pet and stop the bleeding using easily available things such as flour, corn starch and quick-stop.

If your pet is scared, you will have to work your way to get the task done. You can cut the nails of the animal while he is in the bathtub ready for a bath.

You can also keep the animal on a grid like structure. This will allow the legs of the pet animal to fall downwards. This will give you a good grip to cut the nails.

2. Bathing the dwarf hamster

As the pet owner, you will be relieved to learn that the dwarf hamster does not require frequent baths.

Some owners prefer to bathe the dwarf hamster once in two to three months. Excessive bathing of the dwarf hamster can dry out his skin, thus it should be done only when required.

Though the animal does not require regular baths, there are some situations where a bath is important. If the pet has soiled his skin, a bath might important.

Similarly, if the fur near the stomach turns yellow, a bath can help. If a health situation such as urine infection demands a bath, you will have to bathe the pet.

To prepare for the animal's bath, you should make sure that the bath tub or the water sink is clean. Fill more than half of the tub with warm water. Place the animal in the tub.

You can use a small cup to bathe the pet animal. You can also use your hands. Take small amounts of water in your hands and put it over the animal.

You should be gentle, but also quick. Take a small amount of shampoo and lather it all over the animal. Avoid sensitive areas, such as eyes and ears. Focus on the stomach area and the fur.

Once enough lather has formed, use your hands to wash away all the shampoo. Make sure all the soap has been washed off. Take out the pet from the tub and place him in a towel or blanket.

You can use kitten shampoo to bathe the dwarf hamster. Dog shampoos should be avoided because they are scented and can have a reaction on the skin of the dwarf hamster.

You can also make use of baby soaps, such as 'Aveeno baby soothing relief'. You can also use oatmeal and water as a cleansing and moisturising agent.

The criteria to choose the shampoo should be that it should moisturize the skin of the dwarf hamster and not render it dry. Make sure to rinse it off completely, else the animal will develop an itch.

You can also put a few drops of oil in the final water rinse for moisturising the skin of the pet. You can use various moisturising oils, such as olive oil, flax seed oil, cod liver oil, vitamin oil and jojoba oil.

Always check the key ingredients of the shampoo or oil that you are using. Dwarf hamsters develop a fatal allergy due to tea tree oil, so make sure you never use a product containing the oil.

Few dwarf hamsters have the habit of littering in the bath. To avoid this situation, you should make sure that the pet litters in his litter box just prior to the bath.

Also, some dwarf hamsters are scared of running water. You should make sure that the water is not running when you are bathing the pet. Fill the sink or tub before you begin the bath.

Foot bath

Giving a full bath to the dwarf hamster is not an easy job. While it is difficult, it is also not very good for the dwarf hamster. The pet can get dry skin, which can further lead to many skin related problems.

More often than not, the pet owner is forced to give a bath to the dwarf hamster because he has soiled his feet in poop. If you don't clean the feet, the dwarf hamster can soil other areas and can also get an infection.

If you are trying to get rid of the problem of poopy boots, then you can give a foot bath and let go of the full bath.

For a simple foot bath, fill a water tub or sink with over half an inch of water. Make the pet walk in the tub or sink. This will help him to get rid of the poopy boots.

You can also wet a big towel or a paper towel and make the dwarf hamster walk on it. You can also use baby wipes if you want to get rid of dirt or a little amount of grime. This is a simple way to avoid a full dwarf hamster bath.

Conclusion

Thank you again for purchasing this book!

I hope this book was able to help you in understanding the various ways to domesticate and care for dwarf hamsters.

A pet is like a family member. It is more than important that you take care of all the responsibilities for the animal. It is important to have a thorough understanding about the animal. Spend some time to know everything about the dwarf hamster. This will help you know your pet better. The more you know about your pet, the better bond you will form with him. Whenever you get a pet home, you have to make sure that you are all ready for the responsibilities ahead.

A dwarf hamster is an adorable pet that will keep you busy and entertained by all its unique antics and mischiefs. It is said that each animal is different from the other. Each one will have some traits that are unique to him. It is important to understand the traits that differentiate the dwarf hamster from other animals. You also have to be sure that you can provide for the animal. So, it is important to be acquainted with the dos and don'ts of keeping the dwarf hamster.

If you are still contemplating whether you want to domesticate the dwarf hamster or not, then it becomes all the more important for you to understand everything regarding the pet very well. You can only make a wise decision when you are acquainted will all these and more. When you are planning to domesticate a dwarf hamster as a pet, you should lay special emphasis on learning about its behaviour, habitat requirements, diet requirements and common health issues.

The ways and strategies discussed in the book are meant to help you get acquainted with everything that you need to know about dwarf hamsters. You will be able to understand the unique antics of the animal. This will help you to decide whether the dwarf hamster is suitable to be your pet. This will allow you take care of your pet in a better way. You should be able to appreciate your pet and also care well for the animal with the help of the techniques discussed in this book.

Thank you and good luck!

References

http://www.nationalgeographic.com

http://dwarfhamsterblog.com/

https://www.thesprucepets.com

https://www.petco.com

https://pethelpful.com

http://thepipsqueakery.org

http://www.petsathome.com

http://dwarfhamsterhome.com

http://www.sciencekids.co.nz

http://www.enchantedlearning.com

https://www.thespruce.com

http://www.tandfonline.com

http://www.nationalgeographic.com

www.wildlifeontheweb.co.uk

http://animaldiversity.org

http://kids.nationalgeographic.com

http://www.awf.org

http://dwarf hamstercare.org

https://animalcorner.co.uk

http://www.sttiggywinkles.org.uk

https://www.lovethatpet.com

http://www.somersetwildlife.org